This one's on me

This one's on me

Jimmy Greaves

READERS UNION
Group of Book Clubs
Newton Abbot 1979

This edition was produced in 1979 for sale to its members
only by the proprietors, Readers Union Limited,
PO Box 6, Newton Abbot, Devon, TQ12 2DW.
Full details of membership will gladly be sent on request

Reproduced and printed in Great Britain
by A. Wheaton & Co Ltd Exeter
for Readers Union

Contents

Illustrations

1

I am an alcoholic

First the man takes a drink,
Then the drink takes a drink,
Then the drink takes the man.
– Old Chinese proverb

My name is Jimmy G. I am a professional footballer and I am an alcoholic.

These words, first spoken by me at a meeting of Alcoholics Anonymous, have helped save my life. Until then, drink was slowly killing me. I turned to the AA in desperation and found a lifeline that is pulling me back from the road of self-destruction.

The help I needed came too late to save the break-up of a marriage that had been marvellous for most of its twenty years and too late to stop me destroying the foundations of a thriving business career that I had built up for myself outside football.

Now, day by day, I am building a new life for myself and I want to share my experiences – the good and the bad – with other people in the hope that it can help them avoid making the mistakes that wrecked me. In particular, I want to reach any young footballers who could quite unknowingly be on the same downhill course that took me to a hell that defies description.

I am not writing this book for profit. Any money I make will be taken by the taxman to clear Inland Revenue debts that mounted while I was hitting the bottle. Talking openly about my problems will be therapeutic for me and if what I have been through opens the eyes of just one potential alcoholic or brings comfort and hope to anybody already hooked on the habit then all the misery and suffering I have undergone will at least not have been entirely pointless.

Every alcoholic has his own rock bottom. For many, it is the Thames Embankment and a diet of methylated spirits and the ravaged remains of other people's left-overs. The only thing that saved me from the Embankment was that I was always in a position to afford, for the want of a better word, *good* booze and I also had the physical fitness to be able to quickly recover from even the severest bouts of drinking.

My personal rock bottom came in the early hours of a frosty winter's morning when I was ransacking the dustbin in my back garden for empty vodka bottles that had been thrown away by my wife. It was in the winter of 1977. Don't ask me to put times and dates on events of the last five years because the one thing that has been permanently damaged by drink is my memory. I have almost total recall of everything that happened in my football career but there is some sort of mental blockage on the most horrendous moments of my drinking bouts.

But I do have a nightmare memory of the moment I realised that I was a hopeless alcoholic. I had been sleeping a boozing session off in an armchair in the lounge when my wife, Irene – now my ex-wife, I'm sad to say – found my hidden hoard of vodka and in a rage poured all the drink down the sink and threw the bottles into the dustbin. I woke up with a raging thirst, turned cupboards and drawers upside down in a maniacal search for my drinks and finished up kneeling by the side of the dustbin draining the last drops out of the bottles. This was the gutter point of my life.

It looked then like the point of no return. I was having to drink a half-bottle of vodka before I could even get out of bed to face the day. My hands would shake uncontrollably and all I could think about was the next drink. When the pubs opened I would be standing on the doorstep. My first order would be a pint of Guinness, because at least that was nourishing and my only food of the day ...

Wait until the barman turns his back, Jimbo boy. Don't let him see you've got the shakes. That's better. Now I'll have just one more pint before I go to the office ...

By the end of the day I would have got through twelve, thirteen or fourteen pints. No bother. And I could hold my drink so well that only people really close to me would know that I had been on the booze. Then it would be home to a bottle, sometimes two bottles, of vodka.

I am not putting these statistics down to be dramatic or sensational. I just want you to know and understand how bad my problem had become. The wonder is that I am alive to talk about it. Many's the time I have driven home heavily under the influence. Once I even had a police patrolman wake me up in my car where I had fallen into a drunken sleep over the wheel. I told him I had stopped driving because I had felt sleepy. He advised me to drive with my window open and sent me off home with a warning about dangerous parking. I deserved to have been locked up.

At these peaks, or should I say depths, of my problem I was beginning to hurt and embarrass those nearest and dearest to me. But I was so lost in the world of drink that I could not see the damage I was causing. That's the worst thing about the disease of alcoholism. It not only affects the victim but those around him. Now, in my sober state, I can look back and fully realise the anguish and agony I heaped on my family and closest business associates. There were periods of deep depression when I would become violent and abusive at home, wrecking things in wild rage. At my business, I lacked concentration and the total commitment my partners and employees were entitled to expect.

All I can do now, and it's a pretty empty gesture, is apologise from the bottom of my heart for all the misery I caused them and ask if not their forgiveness then at least their understanding. This plea goes particularly to Irene, who was a good wife and a marvellous mother. She took as much as any human being could before finally divorcing me. There was nobody else involved in our break-up. The only co-respondent was the bottle.

What a bloody fool you've been, Jimbo. All you can hope is that Irene understands that you were suffering from an illness. Charles Jackson once wrote a book about an alcoholic called Lost Weekend. *For me, it's been more like five lost years ...*

Thank God, I have got four well-adjusted kids who have managed to come through the crisis I caused a little shaken but unscarred. They have all got good strength of character and I am closer to them now than ever before. I have two beautiful grown-up daughters and two smashing, sports-daft sons and I spend as much time as possible with them. I live on my own in a self-contained flat these days but go home as often as I like. I will always be welcome provided I am not under the influence and somehow out of the wreckage Irene and I – particularly Irene – have kept the family environment alive.

Don't think I didn't try to beat the problem before it got completely out of control. I've had sessions with four top psychiatrists, have been in and out of expensive private clinics at least a dozen times and in the end finished up on the National Health in the alcoholic ward of a mental hospital in Warley, Essex, where they said they could do no more for me after I had been taken helplessly drunk into their care for the umpteenth time.

Why did I start drinking? How did it get out of control? I have asked these questions of myself dozens of times. There is the old theory that alcoholics drink to try to forget. I could come in here with the old joke that I have forgotten what I'm trying to forget. But believe me there is nothing funny in what I have been through.

To an outsider, it must have looked as if I had everything

going for me. International footballer, successful businessman, happily married with four great kids, a marvellous house
and surrounded by admiring friends. But if you delve deeply
into the life and times of Jimmy Greaves you will find the
answers as to why I turned to the bottle for comfort and
escape. It was an escape into hell.

When I was just nineteen, Irene and I were devastated by
the sort of cruel blow that for a long while left me hating the
world. Our first son, Jimmy Greaves Jnr, died of pneumonia
at the age of four months. I had been brought up a Roman
Catholic but from that moment on I started to question everything I had ever been taught and told about God and the
Church. These days I am spiritually stronger than I have ever
been in my life but I still want to scream with anger, frustration
and sheer inner pain when I think back to that tragedy. It left
a deep, lasting scar on both Irene and me.

Within weeks of our losing our darling Jimmy I was pitched
into a traumatic transfer drama that had so many sensational
twists and turns that it was a wonder I stayed sane. It involved
a move to Italy and into a world in which I found I needed
drink to help blot out the nightmare I was living. I spent four
months in Milan. It seemed like a lifetime. I was a kid when
I went out there and felt like an old man by the time Spurs
rescued me.

While with Spurs I drank heavily to help relieve the pressure
of big-time football. My career covered an era when the game
suddenly went sick and defeat became a dirty word. We used
to get really stoked up for the games, with our adrenalin
pumped so high that a lot of us needed the calming influence
of an after-match drink to bring us back down to earth. I
always had the reputation of being a cool, nerveless customer
on the pitch while in actual fact I am the nervy, jumpy type
who smokes like a trooper to control the old jitters.

Drinking was no problem at Spurs. I did it because I liked
it. By the time I joined West Ham I was into the early stages
of alcoholism where I drank because I *needed* to.

The real drinking when I put my life in danger started after

I retired from League football at the comparatively young age of thirty-one.

Too late, I realised I had got off the football bandwagon while I still had years of playing time left in me. In my frustration at having let the good times go, I turned to the bottle. In no time at all the bottle had turned on me. I was a slave to drink.

In the winter of 1977 I was taken to the alcohol unit of a mental hospital in Colchester, Essex. I was drunk out of my head and I was warned then that I was slowly but surely killing myself. I looked around the mental home at other patients with their haunted, staring expressions and got the fear at the back of my mind that my stay could become a permanent residency. I discharged myself after one night.

A few weeks later I was again taken drunk to a mental hospital, this time at Warley. Fleet Street ferreted out the fact that I was having problems and it was after the story of my trouble had been made public that I realised I was at my rock bottom.

I had been an undisciplined member of Alcoholics Anonymous for two years but decided that now I had to have a real go at following their code of living or surrender my life to the bottle.

Prominent in my thoughts at that time was the haunting knowledge that right through my football career I had been compared with a Scottish goal-scoring genius called Hughie Gallacher who, like me, had at one time played for Chelsea.

Gallacher had a drinker's reputation when his playing days finished and his marriage ended in divorce. At the age of fifty-four, forgotten and friendless, he stepped off a platform into the path of a train and was killed.

They said I scored goals like Gallacher. Was I going to follow in his path all the way to the graveyard? The thought became something of an obsession and when everything was going to pieces around me I used to make sure I stood at the back of railway platforms in case I got the sudden urge to run forward and end it all under a train.

Suicidal thoughts were not new to me. In my blackest depressions I would take hold of a razor blade and hold it against my wrists. But I was too sensible or too cowardly, call it what you will, to do more than wonder what it would be like to make the final cut. I was a very sick man.

But I was luckier than Gallacher. I had friends and people around me who cared. The dearest among them was Norman 'Speedie' Quicke and his lovely wife, Jean. Norman is a Fleet Street sports photographer who has been one of my closest pals for more than twenty years. He and Jean were always on hand to help nurse me through my most desperate periods and they were the people Irene would turn to for help when I was getting out of control at home.

Another good pal who has helped me through my self-inflicted pain barrier was Dave Underwood, the chairman of Southern League club Barnet, for whom I am proud and privileged to play during the football season.

In a bid to beat my drink problem, I had made a semi-serious playing comeback with Brentwood and then Chelmsford but finally turned to full-time drinking. Then Dave Underwood gently coaxed me back into the game because he knew that if I broke completely with football that was Jimmy Greaves finished. But for football, I would now be a broken, besotted wreck of a man.

My problem is now common knowledge at Barnet. Throughout football, in fact. I am not proud to be known as an alcoholic but it suits me to have it out in the open. It gives me the challenge that I need. The eyes of the world are on me and I must prove to everybody – particularly to myself – that I have the courage and the character to conquer my problem.

You never recover from alcoholism. Unfortunately it never becomes a 'wasm'. Once an alcoholic, always an alcoholic. But if you can stay sober for the next 24 hours, you can start to bring it under control.

Take each day as it comes, Jimbo. All you have to do is get through the next twenty-four hours without a drink. Today, I shall be sober....

People often ask how you become an alcoholic. There's only one answer. Plenty of practice! A lesson I have learned since becoming a member of Alcoholics Anonymous is that 'one drink is too many and twenty is not enough'. There are three stages of rehabilitation, one leading to the other. AA members know them as the three A's:

1) ADMISSION   2) ADJUSTMENT   3) ACHIEVEMENT

I have cleared the first hurdle which is possibly the hardest for many alcoholics to face. And that is the admission of being an alcoholic.

My name is Jimmy G. I am a professional footballer. And I am an alcoholic.

2

The first drop

Whoe'er has travelled life's dull round,
Whate'er his stages may have been,
May sigh to think he still has found
The warmest welcome at an inn.
– William Shenstone (1714–63)

One of the toughest things about trying to control and conquer alcoholism is that you have to abandon for ever something that has given you so much pleasure. It's not just the drinking that I miss but the atmosphere and environment of a pub. Let's face it, I *enjoyed* becoming an alcoholic.

From way back in my days as an apprentice professional at Chelsea I have loved the camaraderie and companionship of the bar-room. It was only in later years (when the drink had taken the man) that I could not have cared less about the surroundings but only about the contents of my glass.

I was a modest drinker in my youth. A couple of light ales and I was anybody's. Thinking back I now realise it was not a lack of thirst but a scarcity of money that prevented me from indulging myself more in the procession of pubs that run off the King's Road. My wages when I married Irene at the age of eighteen were £17 a week in the season and £8 during the summer. We lived in a one-roomed flat at Wimbledon Football Club and to help pay the rent I used to 'weed' the terraces during the close-season.

It was while at Chelsea that I developed a drinking habit but it was certainly never a problem. The first time I can ever

9

remember being drunk was the day I got married in 1957 and that was not caused so much by quantity as by quality. I was strictly a beer man in those days and the whiskies and brandies that went down my throat before and after the ceremony went straight to my head. It was several years before I became a 'shorts' man.

In those days footballers just couldn't afford to go on the razzle. From what I have seen, the young players of today drink a lot more than during my teenage-to-early-twenties period. We used to be pint sinkers but now the orders are more likely to be Bacardi-and-cokes or gin-and-tonics. I have seen them pay out in a single round what I used to earn in a week at Chelsea.

There is no harm whatsoever in young sportsmen drinking in moderation. A relaxing hour in a pub with your team-mates after a hard match or tough training session can be the best possible wind-down and escape valve from the immense pressures of modern football. But I beg any player who senses that he is perhaps hitting the bottle harder than most to please, please, please learn from my nightmare experiences. Alcoholism is a cunning disease. It creeps up on you without your knowing and suddenly you are hooked. I was one of those who thought it couldn't happen to me. I thought I could switch off my drinking habit any time I wanted to. But when I tried the switch I found the one thing in the world I could not do without was a drink.

Chelsea figured in my life before the days of wine and roses. What carefree times they were, both on and off the pitch! The manager at Stamford Bridge then was Ted Drake, a lovely bloke who will always be remembered for once scoring seven goals for Arsenal in a First Division match at Aston Villa. Ted had been bitten by the youth bug following the success of Manchester United's Busby Babes and used to send out a Chelsea team that was little older than a group of boy scouts. We were labelled 'Drake's Ducklings' and had more potential than any team I have ever played for. But you need experienced players to help draw out the potential and we were just a bunch of kids playing it off the cuff and often coming off second best.

We used to have the most ridiculous results. I recall our once losing 6–5 and can still see Frank Blunstone flinging his boots across the dressing-room afterwards and complaining bitterly to the defenders, 'If we scored eight you could bet on you lot letting in nine.' Nobody disputed it.

It was like being at Butlin's, a real holiday camp atmosphere. Our lack of success did nothing to harm the dressing-room spirit and even in defeat you would find us falling about laughing at things that went on at the club. We were still kids waiting to grow up.

One of the best laughs I had while at Chelsea was during a League match with Everton after they had scored *against* us. Actually we scored it for them and I still rate it one of the all-time unforgettable goals. If there had been action-replay machines around in those days I am sure they would still be showing it as a comedy classic. A long shot from an Everton player slipped under the body of our England inter-national goalkeeper Reg Matthews. Reg scrambled up and chased after the ball, hotly challenged by our big, bold captain Peter Sillett who thought he had a better chance of clearing it. They pounded neck and neck towards our goal. Reg won the race and then, instead of diving on the ball, elected to kick it away. He pivoted beautifully and cracked the ball dead centre – straight into the pit of Peter Sillett's stomach. The ball rebounded into the back of the net and Peter collapsed holding his stomach. The rest of us players collapsed in laughter.

Big Peter was one of the great characters of the team. And what a drinker! He could sink pints until the cows came home and show no ill effects at all. I never used to be able to keep pace with him during our after-match drinking sessions at Chelsea. But drinking never became a problem for him. Heavy drinkers are not necessarily alcoholics. One of the best defini-tions I have heard of an alcoholic is that it is somebody who uses alcohol to such an extent that it interferes with their way of life. A heavy drinker knows when he has had enough. An alcoholic cannot stop, even though he (or she) knows it is having a disastrous effect on his health and social and business life.

I had a recent reunion at Hereford with my old mate Peter Sillett and his brother, John. We had some good laughs about the mad, good old days at Chelsea. John reminded me of a match we played against Preston when I scored a hat-trick to put us 3–0 in the lead. I was a bit of a Jack the lad then and arrogantly informed my team-mates, 'I've done my bit ... now you lot have a go. I'm finished for the day.' By the time we were halfway into the second-half Preston had pulled back to 3–3 and Peter Sillett said, 'Come on, Jim, you'll have to make a comeback.' I scored a fourth goal and then went into my shell again. Preston made it 4–4 and Peter pleaded, 'Just one more, Jim. That's sure to finish them off.' I duly scored a fifth to give us a 5–4 victory at Deepdale. Like I say, my memory isn't what it was and so I looked up the newspaper cuttings and, sure enough, on 18 December 1959, Chelsea won 5–4 at Preston. Greaves five goals. And that victory knocked Preston off the top of the table.

To give you an indication of how the status of professional footballers has changed, I was one of the few players in the Chelsea side with a motor car. I bought my first car, a 1937 Opel convertible, for £30 from my brother-in-law. In those days as long as you had a provisional licence and L-plates up you could drive unaccompanied. I had never driven in my life but somehow steered it right across London to home after collecting it for the first time.

After that I progressed to a 1938 Standard '8' and that became like a team bus with all the players trying to crowd in it after training and matches while we headed for the nearest pub for a pint. I drank no more, no less than most other players then. To me a pint was the reward for a job well done.

It was in those years at Chelsea that I first became aware that perhaps our football wasn't quite so snow-white and free of corruption as I had always liked to believe. I heard whispers and rumours of occasional matches being 'bent' but the only time I was involved in a bribery attempt was when Nottingham Forest were struggling against relegation.

Peter Sillett called us to a players' meeting in what used to be the billiards room above the Chelsea offices at Stamford Bridge. He looked in need of a pint as he told us that one of the Forest players had said there would be a good bonus for us if we let them have both points. We kicked the idea straight into touch and sent Peter to tell Forest that there was no deal.

Typically of us we went and lost the game anyway and at the end of that season Forest finished above us – but we just missed relegation.

I must stress that this was the only time I had any positive first-hand proof of any attempted result-fixing in English football and I was choked for my profession a few years later when it was proved that several leading players had been involved in fixing matches. I felt particularly ill for two old mates of mine, Peter Swan and Tony Kay, both of whom were kicked out of the game at the peak of their outstanding careers. What they did was wrong but I considered the punishment far too severe.

And it was at Chelsea that I had my first experience of 'tapping', which is the football 'in' word that describes an illegal approach by a club for a player. Newcastle were the club and I was the player.

I was pulled on one side by a Newcastle official before a League match against them at Stamford Bridge. He told me I could have £1000 in my hand and a car salesman's job if I would join Newcastle.

That was a lot of money in those days before the lifting of the £20 maximum wage and the salesman's job – a front of course – would have netted me an extra £50 a week. But I had my eyes on another club. In another country. AC Milan were sounding me out and I was a very interested listener.

The days of vino and roses were about to begin. And so were my problems.

3

Days of wine and woes

Then trust me, there's nothing like drinking
So pleasant on this side the grave;
It keeps the unhappy from thinking,
And makes e'en the valiant more brave.
– Charles Dibdin (1745–1814)

I can pinpoint the day, the hour, the minute, the second that
I doomed myself to a life as an alcoholic. It was the moment
I signed my name to a contract that tied me head and foot
to AC Milan. From the day that deal was clinched, I was on
the downhill run. Suddenly I was a little boy lost and confused
in the world of big football business and I began to use drink
as a crutch. Over a period of about a year I was in a state
of turmoil. Frightened, frustrated, bored, aggravated, depressed. All the classic ingredients that drive a man to drink.

It was years later that I became alcoholic in my consumption
and total dependence on drink. But the traps had been set.
It was during the months immediately preceding my move to
Milan and the four torturous months spent in Italy that I
began to convince myself that I could cope more easily with
my problems if I had a drink inside me.

*Sod 'em. Let's go and have a few beers, Jimbo. That'll make
me feel better. The drinks won't make my problems go away
but they'll seem less worrying once I've got a couple of pints
inside me...*

Now, older, wiser and gallons of booze later, I have learned that alcohol is not a stimulant like many people believe but a sedative. It carries you off into a false world, weakening your self control and dulling the faculty of self-criticism. This leads to a loosening of the tongue and produces an outpouring of conversation and laughter that masquerades as stimulation. By making a study of alcoholism I have gleaned that the gaiety and liveliness of those people on their fourth or fifth drink is brought about by the sedative action of alcohol that 'dopes' the higher control centres of the brain. But when I was a bemused twenty-year-old kid caught up in the web of a nightmare transfer deal, I knew nothing of these things. First the man takes a drink ...

To better understand why it all became too much for me to handle without the crutch of a drink, you will need to come back with me to the winter of 1960 when I first asked Chelsea for a transfer. I did not have Italy in mind when I made my request for a move. All I wanted was to get to a club that could match my ambitions. Chelsea, at that time, were something of a joke.

As I remember it, Joe Mears, the late chairman of Chelsea and one of football's great gentlemen and administrators, was the first person to mention the possibility of an Italian job. He telephoned me about a week after I had put in my transfer request and said there was a chance of my going to Italy because an embargo on foreign players was about to be lifted there at the end of the season. Mr Mears, whose son, Brian, is now the very able chairman of Chelsea, wanted to know if I would be interested.

Italy! At the time it was like somebody saying, 'Would you like a share in a gold mine?' I was earning the maximum £20 a week while in Italian football players were picking up small fortunes. Interested? My Italian vocabulary didn't reach much farther than 'spaghetti bolognese' but I was ready to shout 'Si! Si! Si!' all the way to the bank! I was a married man with a daughter and a second baby on the way. Twenty pounds a week was not going to pay for the bright future I had mapped out for my wife and family. Irene and I had already been

15

through hell together. Just a few weeks earlier Jimmy, our beautiful four-month-old son, had died of pneumonia. It was a nightmare experience that nearly drove Irene and me out of our minds. A move to Italy sounded just the change of scenery and surroundings we needed. 'Interested, Mr Mears?' I said. 'When does the plane leave?'

Mr Mears swore me to secrecy. My impression was that he did not want to sell me but if I was determined to go then at least in Italy I could not cause any embarrassment by banging in goals for a rival club.

Anyway, I was happy to keep the prospect of going to Italy under wraps when, right out of the blue, I was approached by an Italian journalist acting as an 'undercover' agent for an Italian club. It was a right back-door effort, the sort of wheeling-dealing approach that I later discovered was the common Italian way of doing business. But I agreed to have unofficial talks with him because I had now been hooked on the idea of going to Italy and I wanted to be in on the start of any deals involving me.

The journalist said he was approaching me on behalf of a certain club. He refused to name them but talked about the sort of deal there could be in it for me. It sounded out of this world. Our next meeting was in a Soho restaurant and this time the Italian agent revealed that he was representing A C Milan. I had done a lot of thinking in between the two meetings and had decided this had to be played straight with Chelsea. I advised the journalist to tell Milan to make a direct approach to my club. We may have been slaves in those days but at least we tried to be loyal to our masters.

Chelsea and Milan had hush-hush talks and the next thing I knew I had to report to an Italian hospital in the heart of London for a medical check-up. This, of course, was all on the quiet. If any of my friends had seen me in hospital they would have thought I was undergoing an autopsy. The things they did to me! They inspected my blood, my urine, my sight, my reactions and every bone in my body including bones in places where I didn't know I had places!

They took about fifty X-rays during my two days in the hospital and at the end of it all the Milan representatives shook their heads and looked doubtful and mournful as if there was no hope for the patient. Apparently a couple of small bones in the small of my back had broken when I was a kid and had interlocked while mending. The Italians reckoned this made me a very dodgy investment. Their fear was that my back would give me trouble later in my career. As it happened, they should have been more concerned about my elbow.

This hospital revelation frightened the life out of me. I had visions of being in a wheelchair before I was thirty. Then a Harley Street specialist studied the X-ray plates and delivered the considered verdict that hundreds of people were walking around with the same bone abnormality. He said Milan need have no fears. I was passed 100 per cent fit and everything was set for me to sign.

Giuseppi Viani, Milan's manager, came to London to clinch the deal. I was offered £10,000 as a signing-on fee. This would be paid over my three-year contract at £3000 a year with a £1000 down payment in my hand the moment I signed the contract. It may not seem a vast amount in these inflationary times but you must remember that with the maximum wage set-up it would have taken me ten years to earn that much in English football.

Chelsea's consolation for selling me was £80,000. Not a bad profit on a player who had cost them just a £10 signing-on fee. It was then a record for an English club although Turin were soon to top that figure when buying Denis Law from Manchester City for £100,000.

Senor Viani talked numbers like a bingo caller. He told me I could earn at least £5000 a year with Milan on top of the signing-on bonus payments. Their basic wage was only about £20 a week but they had huge bonus incentives. The only thing he conveniently forgot to mention was their fining system that cost me hundreds of pounds once I got to Italy.

Anyway, I signed the contract that was to bind me to Milan although for the remaining few months of the season I was

17

to continue to play for Chelsea until the Italian embargo on foreign players was lifted. I got my £1000. Chelsea got a £10,000 down-payment. For Milan it was like putting a deposit on an item of furniture. I had the Chippendale legs.

The signing of the contract took me into one of the worst years of my life. And little did I know it then but it also put me on the long and winding road to alcoholism.

There was a smell of revolution in the air in English football at about the time I was making my decision to go to Milan. League footballers, led by the then players' union chairman Jimmy Hill, were pressing for a new pay deal. The Football League had tossed out a demand for an increase in the £20 maximum wage and the players were in the mood for strike action.

I was a passionate advocate of the players' union case for a new deal and even after signing for Milan attended meetings in London where there were strike threats that would have stopped the League ball rolling. But my old mate Jimmy 'The Beard' Hill, showing the eloquence that has since made him a nationwide television personality, put the players' case so well that the League bosses capitulated and conceded that in future there would be only a *minimum* wage. The soccer slaves had at last escaped their shackles.

I felt delighted for everyone in the game but was sick as a parrot for myself. The fact that Denis Law, Joe Baker, Gerry Hitchens and I had taken the lire bait helped the players clinch the New Deal. The League bosses were frightened of a mass exodus and so gave in. Johnny Haynes, then the England captain, was on the Italian wanted list but Fulham chairman Tommy Trinder boldly announced: 'Johnny Haynes is a top entertainer and will be paid as one. I will pay him £100 a week to play for Fulham.'

In my opinion, this was the funniest line Tommy Trinder ever delivered and my good pal Johnny Haynes was laughing all the way to the bank.

*What have you gone and done, Jimbo? Here I am going all
the way to bleedin' Italy to earn what I can suddenly get in
England. Sod this for a lark. I'm going out for a drink ...*

I had got involved with Milan for mercenary reasons.
Money was the only motive. I wanted to play football in Italy
like I wanted a hole in the head. I had allowed myself to be
seduced by the promise of sudden wealth but in passing judgement on me remember that I was a mere twenty-year-old when
Milan first hooked me.

My immaturity showed in the way I reacted to receiving the
£1000 signing-on fee from Milan. I immediately went out and
blew it on a year-old Jaguar. What a flash git I must have
appeared to onlookers.

I tried everything possible to wriggle out of the Milan deal,
particularly when Joe Mears told me Chelsea would be willing
to pay me £100 a week to stay at Stamford Bridge. Jimmy Hill,
my then adviser Bagenal Harvey, Joe Mears, England
manager Walter Winterbottom and that great administrator
Sir Stanley Rous all put their heads together in an effort to
find a way around my problem. In the company of R. I. Lewis,
a top solicitor, I even went to Italy to plead with Milan for
a cancellation of my contract but they made no secret of the
fact that they would get me banned from ever kicking a ball
again if I backed out of our agreement.

They finally hooked me with the bait they use so well.
Money. They offered me a new contract. This time I was to
receive a £15,000 signing-on fee immediately I put my name
to paper. I would still have preferred to have remained in England but they had me over a legal barrel. So I signed my second
contract at Alassio in June. They paid me £4000 and said I
would get the other £11,000 when I returned from London
in July.

I still wasn't keen on the idea of pulling up my roots and
moving to Italy but I knew I just had to resign myself to it. To
add to my misery, I ended my career with Chelsea in dispute.
My final match was at Stamford Bridge against Nottingham

Forest. I scored four goals and the Chelsea fans carried me around the pitch as if I were the FA Cup. There was hardly a dry eye in the house. Then the club decided they wanted me 'one more time' in a meaningless, end-of-season friendly fixture in Israel. I refused to make the trip and Chelsea slapped a fourteen-day ban on me that deprived me of an England cap in an international match against Mexico at Wembley.

Even now I burn with anger when I think back to that ridiculous suspension by Chelsea. I served them well for four years, scored 132 goals in 169 League matches and then they cashed in on my talent by making a profit of £79,990 on my transfer to Milan. Yet just because I did not want to go on an unimportant tour with them they childishly forced me to finish my career at Chelsea under suspension.

It was enough to drive a man to drink.

Those were the days when I started visiting pubs as a regular habit, a hobby even, rather than as an after-thought. When I was standing at a bar with a pint of beer in my hand it was as if the problems of the Milan Affair would shrink to manageable proportions. Even now, you ask me how to get to any place on the east side of Aldgate Pump out into deepest Essex and I will direct you by pub names. You want to get to Southend from London? From Mooro's – the pub run by my old drinking partner Bobby Moore at Stratford – come up past the Two Puddings on to the A11, past The Charleston, The Thatched House, The Bell and the Red Lion before taking the A12 at the Green Man, Leytonstone. Follow the road down past The George, Wanstead, The Redhouse, Redbridge, Oscars, Newbury Park, and after you have passed The Moby Dick at Chadwell Heath take the flyover at Gallows Corner on to the A127. From here it's a straight run to Southend passing the Fairlane Motel, the Halfway House, the Brighton Run, the Fortune of War and finally The Weir at Rayleigh. No man need die of thirst between London and Southend!

Two particular drinking sprees stand out in my memory from that period. The first was when I was on my way out to Milan to make my debut for them in a prestige friendly against Botafogo in June 1961. They wanted to show me off to their supporters but agreed that I could then return to London to await the birth of our second child which was due to arrive the following month.

I was accompanied on the flight to Milan by *Daily Express* sports columnist Desmond Hackett and photographer Norman Quicke. When they made Des Hackett, The Man With The Brown Bowler, they threw away the mould. He was an astonishing character who brought colour and life to every story he wrote even if – as he often used to say with his tongue in his cheek – 'I never let facts spoil a good story!' Des loved the good life and when we got to Heathrow Airport with two hours to spare before our flight he decided he (or the *Daily Express*) was going to treat me to a lobster and champagne lunch.

We were just finishing off our second bottle of champers and considering starting on a third when Speedy Quicke thought of looking at his watch. 'Our plane,' he informed us, 'left ten minutes ago.'

We caught the next flight out and arrived six hours later than scheduled and at the wrong airport. Thirty miles away on the other side of town at Linate Airport a welcoming committee from AC Milan waited for me with growing impatience and concern. It was just as well they didn't see me stepping off the plane after we had touched down at Malpensa. I am the world's worst flyer bar none. To give myself Dutch courage, I had piled into the champagne cocktails during the flight and was flying pretty high without need of a plane by the time we got to Italy.

I played the next day and scored a goal in a 2–2 draw with the very capable Botafogo team. The fans seemed happy with my performance and the Milan officials said they looked forward to my return in July after our baby had arrived. You could say that was the birth of my problems with the club. The baby – who turned out to be the gorgeous Mitzi – was scheduled to arrive on 15 July and I made provisional plans

to join Milan on 17 July. Mitzi, showing a woman's preroga-
tive, was late and I cabled Milan to tell them I would be staying
with my wife until the baby was born. They showed a great
sense of understanding by threatening to fine me £50 for every
day I failed to make an appearance. From that moment on,
there was no way Jimmy Greaves and AC Milan were going
to get along.

I cabled a reply that regardless of any action that they might
take I was not going to join them until the baby had been born.
This time they accepted the situation but there was already
a bad taste in my mouth.

Mitzi finally deigned to make her appearance on 6 August.
Just by coincidence I bumped into my old Chelsea buddy
John Sillett at the maternity hospital a few hours after Mitzi
was born and we decided to go to the local Old Bell at
Upminster for a drink or two to wet the baby's head. Seven
hours later and in the early hours of the morning we were
happy but legless in the cellar of the Old Bell. The baby's head
was being drowned. We were hiding down in the cellar from
John's mother-in-law who was on the warpath because he was
supposed to have returned home hours earlier.

With a good drink inside me, the problems of Milan seemed
a million miles away. But four days later I at last reported
to my new club. It was the start of a four-month nightmare.
I know it sounds dramatic but I literally became a prisoner
in Milan. The Italian football set-up, as I discovered to my
misery, is totally different to ours. They treat their footballers
like mindless morons, not giving them an inch of trust and
hitting them in the pocket with hefty fines at the slightest hint
of disobedience. I was depressed by the whole scene. Perhaps
if I had been older I might have been able to cope with it.
But had I been older I would have been wiser and never agreed
to have gone there in the first place. I had applied an adolescent
mind to adult problems and kept coming up with the wrong
conclusions.

Between my signing for Milan and then joining them, they
had taken on a new coach, Nero Rocco. He was a big, burly

disciplinarian who had about as much humour as a ruptured bull. Poor old Nero. I made his life hell. And he didn't exactly bring the sunshine of happiness into mine.

Thinking back on it, I feel sorry for Rocco. His job was to get the best out of me for his employers, AC Milan. But I was not interested and went out of my way to make his life difficult. If he had been a different sort of bloke, he might have found a way to melt the ice between us but it seemed the only answer he had for me was to be as tough and cruel a disciplinarian as possible.

As soon as I arrived in Milan I had to join Rocco and the rest of the players for pre-season training in a hideaway camp at Galaratte, which is about forty miles outside Milan. Training camp? It was more like a prison camp. The idea behind having us locked – and I do mean locked – together was to build a team spirit. All I reckoned it did was make the players sick of the sight of each other before a ball was kicked. We were never allowed out of each other's company. It was like one long, boring game of follow-my-leader, with the bullying Rocco out in front barking orders at everybody like a sergeant major. His English was just a little better than my almost non-existent Italian and we used sign language to each other that just about stopped short of Harvey Smith gestures.

We used to have a mass walk-about together after breakfast, followed by a training session in the morning, lunch and then a training session in the afternoon. The rest of the time we spent relaxing together. Always together. We were never allowed outside the hotel unless Rocco was with us and to add to the frustration everything was rationed. Rocco used to order my food and then sit opposite me making sure I ate it. He allowed us only two cigarettes a day, one after lunch and one after dinner. I was a fairly light smoker when I joined Milan but this attempt at dictating when and how many cigarettes I should have simply made me seek out every chance to snatch a crafty smoke.

As for drinking beer, that was considered one of the mortal

sins. Wine was served with our meals but anybody looking for more than one glassful was risking the wrath of the eagle-eyed Rocco. None of the players liked the strict discipline but most of them were so accustomed to it that they just accepted it as their fate. Mind you, they all took every opportunity for crafty cigarettes in the loo or an ice-cold lager at the hotel bar if they were convinced Rocco was not about.

Gianni Rivera, the then Golden Boy of Italian football, watched my consistent rebellion against the system with astonishment bordering on disbelief and once asked me in fractured English: 'Yimmy, why you do these things? Why you fight Rocco all the time? It is surely easier to give in and do as he wants. The money it is good, no?'

I don't think his English was quite good enough to grasp my explanation that I valued my freedom as an individual above everything else. No amount of money could compensate for the loss of it. All my life I have been a non-conformist and throughout my four months in Milan I battled to retain my liberty and individual identity. I had hardly been out there five minutes and I realised there was no way it was going to work.

What with not being able to understand what was being said around me, I quickly got brassed off and homesick. I was on the point of packing my bags and returning home when my solicitor arrived at the training camp to check on my progress. I gave him a real ear bashing and told him exactly how I felt and that I was ready to catch the first available flight out of Milan. 'Three years of this,' I said, 'and they will be locking me away in a mental home.'

My solicitor, a wonderful English gentleman who unfortunately died a few years later in a plane crash, did a good job for me throughout the Milan episode but looking back on it I regret ever having taken legal advice. I think that if right from the off I had just flatly refused to join Milan they would have climbed down. But once I started moving in legal circles my hands were tied. I just had to do everything by the rule-book and my solicitor again explained that my contract was water-tight and that I could not just walk out on Milan. He arranged the next best thing by talking Milan into letting me go home for a couple of days to see my family and friends. Back to good old British beer.

Once home I didn't want to go back but my wife, Irene, knocked that stupid idea out of my head with good common-sense talk. She always has had her head screwed on much tighter than me and she kept me from making silly decisions that I might have regretted later. I returned to Italy for the start of the season and my pal Jimmy Hill, fresh from his triumph in the fight for a New Deal for League footballers, came with me for a few days to help iron out the differences I had with Milan.

But the inevitable split had only been delayed. In my short spell with them – it seemed like a lifetime – I was top scorer with nine goals in fourteen games but I hated every second of the football. The game out there was being strangled to death by stifling defensive systems and we never played with more than two forwards in attack. I was never one for looking for trouble on the pitch but it was so spiteful and vicious that even I was moved to try to kick things other than the ball. The first time I lost my temper was with a player from Genoa who spat in my face after tripping me up. I responded by kicking him in the shins for which the referee awarded Genoa a free-kick. They scored from it and Rocco went berserk over my retaliation. He punished me the only way he seemed to know how – with a fine.

My brother-in-law Tom and his wife, Nancy, brought Irene out to join me and things looked a little brighter until I discovered I was still a prisoner. We had a sight-seeing day out at Venice soon after they arrived and for that I was fined £500 for breaking city limits.

Tom knew better than anybody the hell I was going through. On an earlier visit he and I had sat on the balcony of the team hotel late one night knocking back lagers and enjoying a nice relaxed time. One of Rocco's spies reported back to the God-father and the next day two workmen came to my room and

25

nailed planks of wood across the door leading to the balcony. I blew my top and ripped them down.

Rocco became obsessed with getting me to knuckle under and become just another sheep in his flock of highly-paid but unhappy footballers. He used to deliberately sit at the bottom of the stairs in our hotel to make sure I did not sneak out. Tom and I risked death one night to escape him. We climbed out of a window three storeys up and edged along a narrow ledge looking for an escape route, while Rocco was stationed downstairs watching the main exit.

Tom and I were giggling like little boys at the way we had dodged Rocco when we came up against a brick wall. The ledge had led to a dead-end. We finally sneaked out by causing a distraction downstairs, Tom pretending to order enough drinks to keep us occupied in the hotel for the whole night. While Rocco was busy cancelling this enormous order, Tom and I tip-toed out the rear exit. It cost me a fine of about £300 but it was well worth it to get the better of Godfather Rocco.

At this distance, I can accept the criticisms that were being made of me at the time. The English newspapers tagged me as the spoilt young brat of football. A lot of what they said about me was true although they gave the false impression that I was a wealthy young man. Much of my £4000 signing-on fee had been eaten up by legal fees and air fares and Milan, understandably, never did get around to paying me the outstanding £11,000. I was getting fined so often that my wages were sometimes lower even than when I was playing for Chelsea. I was perhaps a young brat but nobody was spoiling me.

The Italian Press murdered me. They could not have done a better assassination job had they been given a contract by the Mafia. Typical of the filth that was being written by their gutter Press was a story that accused me of holding a wild orgy in the flat into which Milan had moved me. This all came about because a reporter had looked into our living-room through binoculars and had seen Irene and Nancy walking about in shorts.

A few days later Rocco and I had a right up and downer,

insulting each other through an interpreter after he had carpeted me for going to the airport to meet Irene on the eve of a match. Italian clubs ban their players from going near wives, girlfriends or anything in a skirt on the day before and after a match. They lock their players away in hotels in a bid to keep sex and soccer apart. But I was an 'old' married man of three years and saw no harm in meeting my wife after she had flown into a strange country. But I suppose Rocco was worried by the 'sex maniac' image the newspapers had given me. He must have had visions of Irene and me running naked along one of the runways of Milan airport.

Tommy Steele, that fine entertainer and football fanatic, dropped in to see me during a trip to Italy. He had heard and read about all my problems and wanted to see for himself the sort of treatment I was receiving. I took Tommy along to an after-match meal and he just could not believe the childish way we were treated. He was appalled by the do-this-do-that discipline that reduced grown men to the role of robots. We were told what we could and couldn't eat, what drink we should have and when we should go to bed ... to sleep, naturally.

'I can get you out of this, Jim,' said Tommy, his eyes alight with enthusiasm. 'I'll hire a private plane, smuggle you aboard as one of my musicians and have you home in next to no time.'

Now Tommy is one of the world's great leg-pullers but he was deadly serious and started to work out exactly how he could spirit me out of Italy. He was all ready to put his escape plan into operation when I heard on the grapevine that my deliberate policy of non-cooperation had at last pushed Milan to breaking point.

They were buying a Brazilian as a replacement for me and turfed me out of my flat and put Irene and me into a pokey little backstreet hotel. There was no way I was going to stand for that and so, at my own expense, I booked us into a five-star hotel where the brigade of British Press boys who had shared many of my experiences were staying.

I was less of a prisoner now and got down to some really serious drinking in the company of the journalists who were a great set of blokes and helped make my miserable stay in Milan a little more tolerable.

We got on so well together and had so many memorable nights out of sight of Rocco and his spies that we formed a Jimmy Greaves Club and each of the reporters who visited me in Milan became members and purchased a special commemorative tie that had a map of Italy overprinted with my initials and a football.

More appropriately, the tie should have shown a wine bottle with the cork exploding. The people with whom I did most of my drinking were the journalists who were filing stories back to England about my 'spoilt brat' antics. I agreed with much of what they wrote and was only too happy to feed them stories about my bust ups with Rocco because I knew Milan would finally get so sick of it all that they would be glad to see the back of me.

Among the members of our exclusive club were Clive Toye, Des Hackett and Speedy Quicke (*Daily Express*), Bill Holden and Ken Jones (*Daily Mirror*), Peter Lorenzo (*Daily Herald*), Maurice Smith (*The People*), Laurie Pignon and Tony Stratton-Smith (*Daily Sketch*), Ian Wooldridge (*News Chronicle*), Peter Moss, Roy Peskett and Brian James (*Daily Mail*), Donald Saunders (*Daily Telegraph*) and Brian Glanville (*Sunday Times*). Believe me, their company kept me sane.

We used to have two regular meeting places right in the heart of Milan, La Tampa Restaurant and a nightclub called Porto Dora. We had many wildly enjoyable evenings together and one sticks out in my memory because it was the night Mr Ian Wooldridge nearly became Miss Ina Wooldridge.

Our topic of conversation, washed down with several pints of beer and a few carafes of wine, had got round to the subject of speed and fitness. Ian, I recall, was particularly outspoken against professional footballers and said something along the lines that even he could run the legs off most of us. It was getting on for two o'clock in the morning when I invited him to put his legs where his mouth was. The other Press boys decided that they, too, would like to prove their athletic prowess and six of us lined up outside the nightclub in the piazza for the start of a 100-yard race.

By the halfway distance I had dropped everybody but Ian who was battling away just a couple of yards behind me. Suddenly twenty yards ahead I saw a spiked chain stretched across the road at about hip height. I slowed down and Ian, thinking he had got the better of me, dashed past like a man going for the winning goal at Wembley. He did about four somersaults after the chain had caught him right where it hurts and we had to pick him up and carry him back to the nightclub for a fortifying drink. He survived to become, in my opinion, the greatest of all English sportswriters. Just think, he very nearly became the first female sportswriter of the year!

I remember a cruel trick that Clive Toye and I played on an Italian-based journalist that will be of particular interest to my old England team-mate George Eastham. Clive, who has since become an influential executive on the US soccer circuit, told me that somebody was feeding stories back to London behind the backs of the other Press boys.

It was Irene, always more perceptive than me, who fathomed it out that it had to be this Italian-based English journalist. One morning Clive and I allowed him to overhear a private conversation we were having in which we fabricated a story that George Eastham was being bought by AC Milan as a playing partner to keep me happy.

The fish took our bait but the joke backfired on Clive. He was awakened in the early hours of the next morning by the *Express* office wanting to know why he had got a whiff of an exclusive *Daily Sketch* story that George Eastham was joining AC Milan for £100,000.

So now George knows the truth about that alleged Milan bid.

It seems like a lifetime ago when I look back over eighteen years to my days in Milan. At this distance a lot of it seemed like good fun but most of the time I was in a badly depressed

29

state. I made myself ill with worry, lost weight and was in a run-down condition.

I was drinking a fair amount but stuck mostly to beer and was young enough to run off hangovers in training. Drinking was certainly not a problem then but it had become an accepted part of my life.

The first I knew for certain that Milan were ready to let me go was when Chelsea chairman Joe Mears and his wife, Betty called to see me during a holiday trip to Italy. They thoughtfully brought us a two-pound bag of tea, although as far as I was concerned a couple of pints of bitter would have been more welcome.

Joe told me that Milan were preparing to offer me for sale and that if I agreed to return to Chelsea they would pay me a guaranteed wage of £120 a week. I told him that naturally I was interested but did not want to build my hopes up because Milan were being so bloody-minded about everything. I had just had a furious row with them because they refused to let me have my passport after a club trip to Yugoslavia. I went to the British Consulate to complain and Milan were ordered to hand it back to me. When I called into the office to collect the passport it was thrown across the room at me. Things had got that bad.

Even on the pitch I was being treated like a leper. I suppose the players blamed me for Rocco's bad moods and refused to pass the ball to me unless it was absolutely necessary. I remember scoring a goal against their bitter rivals Inter-Milan and not a single player came to congratulate me, even though I had waltzed past three defenders before sticking the ball into the back of the net. I trundled back to the centre-circle and turned in the general direction of poor old Rocco and gave him a double reverse V-sign.

Not long after, Milan at last officially announced that they were ready to receive offers for me and Bill Nicholson, the Spurs manager, got word through to me that he was very interested. This was the best bit of news I'd had for months because

Tottenham were the club I rated above all others. They had just become the first club this century to win the League and FA Cup double and the prospect of playing for them was immediately appealing.

Chelsea and Spurs were the two front runners for me and Milan tried to get them locked in an auction. But they were outsmarted by Bill Nicholson and Chelsea secretary John Battersby. They knew what Milan were up to and came to a secret agreement to put in identical bids. Both of them offered £90,000 and then the three of us put our heads together at a private meeting. After a long talk with Bill Nick and John Battersby, I told them that Tottenham was the club I preferred to join.

Battersby agreed to drop out of the bidding so that Spurs could have a clear field. Nick would have done the same for him if I had chosen to return to Chelsea. My old club had been prepared to make me the highest-paid player in Britain at £120 a week but I settled for the £60-a-week offer from Tottenham.

There were two main reasons. One – I felt that returning to Chelsea would have been a backward step, perhaps to the problems I had wanted to escape just a few months earlier. Two – I really fancied playing for that Tottenham team. The thought of it excited me. I reckoned I would be playing with the greatest club team in the history of British football. Nothing has happened since to make me either regret my decision or change my rating of that team.

Anyway, Bill Nick continued the negotiations on his own. He did not want me saddled with the label of the Football League's first £100,000 player and so did a deal at the odd price of £99,999.

Nick took three days hammering out the details of the deal. Two days later I was on my way home.

After getting into my drinking stride in Milan, I can look back at the move to Tottenham as the period in my life when knocking back booze became more than just a habit.

It started to become a necessity, like water to a plant. And I loved every drop of it.

4

The long hot summer

If all be true that I do think,
There are five reasons we should drink;
Good wine, a friend, or being dry,
Or lest we should be by and by;
Or any other reason why.
– Henry Aldrich (1647–1710)

If a man's life is as the four seasons, then there is no question that I had my summertime at Tottenham. During nine fabulous years there I stopped using drink as a crutch. Along with my football, it became pure pleasure.

On the day that I joined Spurs the players were wary of me. They had been reading the day-by-day accounts of my exploits in Italy and must have been thinking that I was nothing but a troublemaker. Having just won the League and Cup double without me, they understandably looked on me as an intruder who could possibly rock their happy and successful boat.

It didn't take me long to kick their doubts into touch and to settle into the side – both on and off the pitch – as if I had been at White Hart Lane all my life. But first of all I had to clear an unnecessary obstacle put in my way by the Football League.

They were flexing their muscles when I made my escape from Milan and held up my official registration with Tottenham pending an investigation. Apparently, they wanted to discover whether I had been offered any under-the-counter inducements to get me away from Italy. They had to be joking! I was the one who would willingly have paid to get the hell out of it and back into English football. The truth is that I was flat broke when I arrived back in England. All I had to call mine was my Jaguar car and I had to pay £500 import duty on that when we arrived at Dover. I raised the money by selling the story of my final break with Milan to a Sunday newspaper. I was so hard up for the next few months that Irene, our two daughters and I had to lodge with my in-laws in a three-bedroomed house in which four adults were already living. Whoever thought I had come back from Milan a millionaire was about a million pounds out in their assumption.

The League inquiry into my transfer took place in a Sheffield hotel. I got the distinct impression that the meeting had been called simply as an excuse for a drink and a chat. League secretary Alan Hardaker seemed the only one remotely interested in asking any meaningful questions and within a matter of minutes they were satisfied that everything had been above board. Bill Nicholson and I had a good chuckle during the train journey home over the performance of one of the League officials who appeared to spend the entire hearing in a deep sleep.

Welcome home, Jimbo. Nothing's changed. Some of the people running the game are still hitting the booze. God, I'd hate to get like that ...

I had made my first appearance for Spurs five days earlier in a reserve match at Plymouth. They had a record reserve attendance at Home Park of 13,000 and Argyle chairman Ron Blindell came on to the pitch with a microphone before the kick-off to welcome me back to English football. I distinctly remember his words as the opposing players lined up to applaud me: 'On behalf of Plymouth Argyle, the people of Devon and Cornwall but not least the whole of England I say to you, welcome back.'

It was unexpected and embarrassing yet also very reassuring. I had taken so much stick in the Press for the way I'd messed Milan about that I thought I might return to a hostile atmosphere. People are swayed by what they read in the news-papers. The pen is mightier than the boot. But the Plymouth fans, bless 'em, really made me feel comfortable and happy to be home. I poked a couple of goals in and everybody was happy afterwards at what developed into quite a drunken marathon.

I went out for an extended drink with Mel Hopkins, Terry Dyson and a couple of other players and then, during the long train journey home, we made so much beer-provoked noise that a passenger complained to a British Railways inspector. We later learned that the man making the protest was a member of the English Rugby Union. In my experience, Rugby players are the noisiest and rowdiest of all sportsmen when in transit. People who live in glass houses . . .

Everything started to slot into place at Tottenham when I made my first-team debut against Blackpool. I got lucky and scored a hat-trick. I have to admit that one of the goals was a bit special. Dave Mackay took one of his long throw-ins, Terry Medwin flicked the ball on and I scored with what the newspapers described as 'a spectacular scissors kick'. From that moment on I was accepted by the Tottenham fans and players as 'one of them'.

Tottenham was not only a great soccer club but also a marvel-lous social club. Several of us gave a lot of attention to our drinking and pubs like the White Hart and the Bell and Hare – both within goal-kicking distance of the ground – became like clubhouses to us.

Now I am not naming names to suggest that any of my team-mates were putting booze before football. In that 'Super Spurs' side of the 1960s, everybody pulled his weight and with all of us football came first. A good drink was our reward for a job well done. Our manager Bill Nicholson and coach Eddie Baily knew that several of us were pretty nifty with our elbows but never really appreciated the full extent of our drinking. As long as we were giving 100 per cent on the pitch and in training, they were content. Anybody who saw that magnificent team in action will know that there was not a single passenger or slacker.

After we had done our work, several of us used to get through some heavy drinking to wind down and lift the pressure after what were physically and mentally demanding matches. Dave Mackay used to be our leader on and off the pitch. Danny Blanchflower was a superb skipper who was all elegance on the park and full of wonderful eloquence off it. Dave was our *physical* leader. He went into battle like a warrior and he tackled his social life with the same exuberance and total commitment. Danny didn't drink at all and so it was Dave who used to take command of our drinking schools in the back room of the Bell and Hare. He would sit up at the bar like a king on his throne and would invariably get in the first order. *Pints all round.*

We would dissect every move in the match. *Pints all round.* Then we'd look ahead to the next match. *Pints all round.* Then we would swap the latest jokes and gossip. *Pints all round.* It didn't seem to be doing us any harm and we knew that we could run it all off next day in training. Even now I would not discourage young footballers from having this sort of after-match wind-down session. But I would advise them to pack up and go home after a couple of pints and certainly never move on to shorts. The secret of keeping drinking under control is to stop at the right time. I thought I knew when I would need to stop but I never saw the red light until it was too late.

Other regulars in our drinking school used to be Cliffie Jones, John White, Bobby Smith and goalkeeper Bill Brown. Alan Gilzean joined us as a newcomer and quickly qualified as a vice-president of our club. He was the only one who could keep pace with Dave Mackay when the going really got tough in our long drinking sessions.

Cliffie Jones and John White were a couple of terrors together, never malicious but always mischievous. They used to be room-mates but became so boisterous that Bill Nicholson had to separate them. I recall an incident after a European

Cup match in Portugal that typifies the way they used to behave together. We were staying in a posh, plush old-style hotel in Estoril and decorating the walls were shields and swords from some ancient Portuguese battle. At the dead of night Bill Nick was summoned from his room by a frantic manager who'd had complaints from guests about clanking noises. Nick went to the landing at the top of the winding staircase to find Jonesie and Whitey in the middle of an Errol Flynn-style fencing duel.

They were two lovable blokes who could be totally irresponsible and continually on the look out for laughs. I was assigned to have John White as my room-mate and in no time at all he was getting me into trouble. Once on the morning of a match against Manchester United at Old Trafford he hung out of our hotel room window three storeys up and started screaming for help. The police were called and that really took some explaining away. But the officers were football fans and let us off with a warning on the understanding that we would get them tickets for the match.

After that, Cliffie Jones became my room-mate and that was enough to drive me to drink. He would come on a tour with little more than a toothbrush. I had a right go at him once when I caught him walking around in my brand new shoes on the beach in Israel. Another time he came down to dinner wearing my England teamsuit. I told him he wasn't good enough to wear it and said that any Welshman who could keep a ball up six times without it hitting the floor automatically qualified for a Welsh cap. That was then far from the truth, of course, because Wales had a whole army of outstanding players like John and Mel Charles, Ivor Allchurch, Roy Vernon and, how could I forget, Cliffie Jones.

I can get very emotional and choked up just thinking back on those glorious days, particularly as dear John White has been taken from us. The day he was struck down by lightning on a golf course was a terrible blow for everybody who had come into contact with that genius of a footballer and rascal of a man. Poor old Jonesie was cut up more than most. John was right at the peak of his career and would have established himself as one of the all-time greats over the next year or two.

When you're slipping into one of your depressions, Jimbo, just think of Whitey and realise how lucky you are ...

I did well with room-mates at Tottenham. My regular companion used to be big Bobby Smith who sadly for him had a gambling sickness that became as difficult to control as my drinking problem. Bobby and I were good pals and I still have a soft spot for the old feller even though he stretched our friendship to the limit with money requests to help him pay off betting debts.

Gambling fever can be as destructive as alcoholism and, like my illness, it hurts those around and close to the victim. Bobby had the betting bug so bad that even when he was abroad with the Tottenham and England teams he would still indulge himself. I would be lying on the bed in our room having an afternoon nap before, say, one of our European Cup matches when suddenly I would hear Smithy shouting down the phone to a bookie in London. 'Is that you, Izzy? Put me twenty on the favourite in the first, twenty on the favourite in the second and I'll have a twenty win double.' Then he would phone back and get the results. He was the most generous bloke walking this earth when he was a winner but unfortunately his losses were greater than his successes. One day in Holland before a match against Feyenoord Bill Nick called us all together in the hotel and said somebody was making telephone calls to London and putting pounds on the Tottenham bill. Before he could say any more, Smithy stood up and shouted, 'All right, keep your shirt on. I'll pay it back when we get home.' The funny thing is that until Smithy's outburst Bill Nick had no idea who was making the calls.

We were surrounded by characters at Tottenham who could have been created by a cockney Damon Runyon or a twentieth-century Charles Dickens. There was Johnny 'The Stick' Goldstein, One Arm Lou, Fat Stan Flashman, all of them ticket touts but larger than life people who gave a richness and colour to life at Tottenham. People looking in from the outside used to dismiss them as hangers-on but in a way they were as much a part of the Spurs scenery as any of the players or officials. It makes me angry when I read of people like Johnny the Stick and die-hard supporters like Morris Keston being described as hangers-on. Both were only too willing to help any Tottenham player on hard times and gave more to Tottenham than they ever took.

Johnny the Stick in particular had a heart of gold. He's dead and gone, God rest his soul, but I've got warm memories of a man who used to live by his wits and was always ready to help anybody who was down. The only illegal activities I've ever got up to in football was feeding the likes of Johnny the Stick with FA Cup tickets for which he would pay a fair price before selling them on the black market where supply and demand dictated the prices. Dear old Johnny used to idolise me as a footballer and even used to sleep in one of my old Spurs shirts. They don't make them like him anymore.

Measuring that Tottenham team in footballing terms, I would say that if they were at their peak today they would be strong contenders for the championship of this country and of Europe. I concede that the present Liverpool team might have mastered them, not because they are a superior side but because they are more miserly and would not have pushed as many men forward as us.

They lack the flair and imagination that set the 'Super Spurs' apart as one of the most *attractive* teams of all time. With perhaps the exception of the Manchester United team of the mid-1960s – when Best, Law, Charlton and Crerand were in full flow – there has not been a side to match Tottenham as a forward-moving combination. We had some defensive deficiencies but when it came to attack we were second to none. Tottenham always *entertained* when they were winning. I'm not sure that can be said of the Liverpool side who have at last pumped some pride back into English football by winning the European Cup twice in succession.

Above all the old Spurs had the right blend. At the back we had Bill Brown, a magnificent goalkeeper on his day. The one problem he never really conquered was cutting out crosses but here he had the good old reliable Maurice Norman to help him out. Big Mo was an ox of a man. Big in build and big in heart. Strangely enough, he was not that good in the air but he was so tall that he usually got to the high balls before rival forwards had started jumping. On those occasions when the otherwise dependable Bill Brown made a mess of a cross you would always find Big Mo thumping the ball away. There have been more skilful and polished centre-halves than Maurice but I have yet to come across one as physically strong as the likeable 'Swedebasher' from deepest Norfolk.

Peter Baker at right-back was very much under-estimated. His hard, uncompromising style balanced perfectly with the more skilled approach of his partner Ron Henry. I can never recall a winger giving Peter a roasting and this was in an era when every team carried two wingers playing wide on the flanks. He could be tough to the point of brutal when necessary and many's the time he ended dangerous raids with perfectly-timed tackles.

I would rate Ron Henry among the top six left-backs I have played with and that includes my England experience. He was a thinking full-back who was perhaps under-rated because he did his work with so little fuss. Ron would always use the ball intelligently and was a master of positional play. It was a pity that he got his one and only England cap in Alf Ramsey's first match as England manager. We got trounced 5–1 by France and unlucky Ron was one of those who carried the can.

Danny Blanchflower was the poet of our team. He gave us style and panache and was a captain in every sense of the word, inspiring us with his almost-arrogant performances and lifting us with words of wisdom. It was a tragedy in my opinion when Tottenham decided against giving him the manager's job in succession to Bill Nicholson. League football would have been all the richer for his appointment because he would have brought vision and inventive ideas to the game, so helping to loosen the straitjacket into which our football has been placed by blinkered coaches. I was delighted that Chelsea had the sense to bring him back into the game at club level. A pity it had to be in at the deep end.

Danny's contribution to the Tottenham team was as important as Bill Nick's. His influence went much farther and deeper than his performances on the pitch. He was the dressing-room tactician, the training-ground theorist, the man who talked up for players during moments of crisis and misunderstanding. Danny rivalled even my old England team-mate Johnny Haynes for firing a pass through the heart of a defence.

He was a great reader of the game and had the courage and intelligence to make tactical decisions in the heat of battle that most people are happy to sort out in the dressing-room inquest when it is too late. I remember a time when Danny virtually over-ruled Bill Nick and gave us a team talk that motivated us into winning the European Cup Winners' Cup. If Bill Nick had a fault it was that he used to worry too much about the opposition. There was always the danger that his concern would spread to us like a contagious disease and eat away our confidence. He was in this sort of morose mood before the Cup Winners Final against Atletico Madrid in Rotterdam in 1963 when we were bidding to become the first team to take a major European trophy back to Britain.

Dave Mackay failed a fitness test shortly before the Final and this really shook Bill, who like everybody else believed in the miracle that was Mackay. He was thoroughly miserable at the pre-match team talk and built Atletico Madrid up as the greatest team he had ever seen. The impression he gave us was that their defenders were as big as mountains and would crush any forward silly enough to go near them. He made their attack sound as if they had five forwards with the skill of di Stefano and the shooting power of Puskas. I knew Bill Nick was trying to avoid any complacency among us but he had overplayed it. He had frightened us to death!

Danny called a secret players' meeting after Nick had finished with us and did a magnificent job repairing our shattered confidence. I wish I'd got what he said down on a tape recorder because it was in the Churchill class as a rallying speech and would have served as a lesson to all managers and coaches how to lift and motivate a team before a vital match. He told us to put ourselves in the place of the Atletico players and to imagine what they were thinking about *us*. We had the reputation of being one of the greatest club teams in the world and Danny, a master at the word game, convinced us that Atletico would be petrified. We won 5–1 and for once I was pleased to see Bill Nick proved hopelessly wrong with his analysis of a team.

If somebody put a gun to my head and insisted that I name *the* greatest player in that great Spurs side it would have to be Dave Mackay. He had just about everything: power, skill, drive, stamina and, above all, infectious enthusiasm.

Power? I have shuddered at some of his tackles on rival players and he used to go in just as hard even after twice breaking his leg. When people talk these days about the hard men of the game I have a little chuckle to myself when I think back to the likes of Tony Kay, Stan Crowther, Maurice Setters, the young Norman Hunter and Nobby Stiles, Stan Lynn ... and so many more players who, if they tackled you, you stayed tackled! Mackay was as tough as any of them and I often offered up a silent prayer of thanks that he was with me and not against me.

When I first came into the game, Bolton were the team everybody feared for their sheer brute force. Their England international full-back Tommy Banks used to say to Chelsea winger Peter Brabrook: 'If thou tries to go past me, lad, thou will get gravel rash ...' And a favourite comment from their rugged half-back Derek Henning, shouted loudly to his defensive colleagues early in the match, was: 'If my inside-forward 'appens to come through, chip him back to me ...'

Believe me, today's so-called hard men are like an army of Andy Pandys when compared with them. Where Dave Mackay was superior to all of them was that he had delicate skills to go with his enormous strength. Bobby Moore is one

41

of the few defenders I can think of who could rival him for ball control in a tight situation. He was the king of the first-time pass, drilling the ball through to a team-mate as accurately and as casually as if in a training stint despite being under pressure from an opponent. Dave took over from Danny as Spurs captain and I can safely say that I played under the two greatest skippers that ever carried a ball on to the pitch.

Terry Dyson and Terry Medwin used to play musical chairs with the no. 7 shirt in that Spurs team. Both were determined competitors who never let the side down. It was a toss up between them but I think Dyson's grit and whole-hearted endeavour just gave him a slight edge over Medwin. Dyson would run his legs off for the team and many times popped up with the vital winning goals. He had the most memorable match of his career in the Cup Winners' Cup Final against Atletico Madrid when he scored two goals and continually had the Spanish defence in total disarray with his thrusting runs. Terry was big enough to admit that he did not have the skill of some of those tremendous players around him but he more than made up for it with his effort.

Medwin was a very correct player, a student of the game who did everything with care and accuracy. He was always a menace to defences with his quick change of pace and used to get up well to head the ball. It is a measure of the strength in depth of that Spurs squad that Medwin could not win a regular first-team place yet played more than 30 times for Wales. He came out of that marvellous Swansea finishing school that also produced players of the calibre of the All-church brothers, Mel Charles, Mel Nurse and, of course, my old mate Cliffie Jones.

John White was a great, great player when he died and I am convinced he was going to get even better. He was so aptly named the Ghost of White Hart Lane. It was his ability off the ball that made him such a phenomenal player. He would pop up from out of nowhere just when he was needed to make a pass or collect the ball. Like Danny Blanchflower he had the gift for being able to give the exact weight to a pass so that the ball would arrive where and when you wanted it. John had the energy to run all day and could cut a defence in half with just one cunningly placed ball. With White together in midfield with Blanchflower and Mackay we just could not go wrong.

Up front with me was my old buddy Bobby Smith, who had the muscle-power to petrify even the bravest defenders. Smithy did not think he was in the game until he had hammered into the goalkeeper in the earliest possible moment in a match. This was in the days when forwards were allowed to make physical contact with goalkeepers. Nowadays, if you so much as breathe on them it is a free-kick and possibly a booking against you. It's made life easier for the goalkeepers and the game less of a spectacle for the fans. I think Bobby would feel redundant in a match if he was playing in the modern game.

Bobby liked to let everybody know who was boss right from the word go. He used to frighten the life out of me with some of his rough, tough methods, particularly against foreign goalkeepers who were not accustomed to his sort of treatment on the continent. Many's the time I've seen Continental goalkeepers freeze at the sight of the mighty Smith powering towards them like a galloping carthorse.

He also used more subtle methods to get a psychological advantage, such as a muttered curse and raised fist or just a cold-eyed stare that would have had even Muhammad Ali flinching! We were coming off the pitch against Bratislava in a European Cup Winners Cup first leg match after losing 2–0 when Bobby saw to it that we would win the return match in London. He made an 'I'll have you at home' gesture to the centre-half who had been giving him a bit of a rough time. Then he put a clenched fist under the goalkeeper's nose and said with a heavy Yorkshire accent: 'Londres ... Londres ... You'll get yours in Lon-dres ...' It may have lost something in its interpretation but the message was not lost on the goalkeeper who literally turned white. He knew what was coming and Smithy didn't disappoint him. He charged the goalkeeper into the back of the net in the first minute and the poor bloke lost all his appetite for the game. We knocked six past him because he was always too busy looking for Smithy coming at him to worry about the ball!

Because of his huge physical presence, Smithy tended to get labelled as a clumsy player. But he had a load of finesse and was exceptionally skilful at laying the ball off. He and I struck up a terrific partnership for England and Spurs and I feel that Bobby was never given the full credit he deserved for helping my goal haul. If Joe Jordan is worth £350,000, then I reckon Smithy – had he been playing today – would have been valued at twice that amount. He was that great a centre-forward.

Out on the left – and sometimes the right – wing we had the amazing Cliffie Jones who, at his peak, was without question one of the world's greatest wingers. When he was in full flight I doubt if there was a more dangerous forward on the ball. He used to run with the pace, determination and bravery of a Welsh wing-threequarter. There were times when I used to wonder if he knew exactly where he was going as he went past a succession of defenders on diagonal runs and I used to tease him after matches by telling him he had beaten me three times on the way to the bye-line. He was just about the fastest thing on two feet and it used to amuse everybody but him the way he would skid face first along the turf after a trip. It was the only way defenders could bring him down because he was too quick for them to catch with a tackle.

Jonesie was brave to the point of madness in the penalty area where he would think nothing of diving in with his head where most players would think twice about putting a boot. He used to rise like a salmon at the far post to head spectacular goals that were remarkable when you realise he was a smallish bloke with a slim frame. When you talk about great wingers like Matthews, Finney and Best you should include Jonesie in that bracket. He was certainly as effective as any of them.

Cliffie – who comes from a famous sporting family that includes former Welsh international Bryn Jones and top sports columnist Ken Jones – is passionately proud of his Welsh heritage and I used to take great delight in singing 'Land Of Our Fathers' in the Tottenham dressing-room after we had hammered Wales in Home International matches. It was the only time chirpy Cliffie used to be lost for words.

All the booze I've drunk may have damaged my memory but I am ready to argue with anybody that this Tottenham team was one of the – if not *the* – best club team in post-war British football. I get goose pimples just thinking about some of the football we used to play. It was out of this world.

When Dave Mackay was carried off on a stretcher with a broken leg at Old Trafford one cold December night in 1963, the heart of the Tottenham team went with him. Looking back, it was as if the team died overnight. Of course, it took more than a season for the complete break-up of the side but somehow we were never the same again after Dave had been injured in a collision with Noel Cantwell that must have left the Manchester United skipper wondering about the validity of his challenge.

Danny Blanchflower was already on his way out with a recurring knee injury and at the end of the season John White was tragically killed by lightning on a North London golf course. We had lost the three most vital cogs in our machine.

Bill Nick got busy in the transfer market and bought Alan Mullery from Fulham, Laurie Brown from Arsenal, Cyril Knowles from Middlesbrough, Pat Jennings from Watford, Jimmy Robertson from St Mirren and Alan Gilzean from Dundee. He took a breather and then went shopping again, this time bringing in Mike England from Blackburn and Terry Venables from Chelsea.

Nick was trying to build another 'Super Spurs'. He never quite made it. The new Tottenham team had some great moments together but we never touched the peak performances of the Blanchflower–White–Mackay era.

I was sick that Bill Nick failed in his bid to bring Johnny Haynes to Tottenham as John White's successor. Haynesie and I had an almost telepathic understanding at England level.

We could read each other like a book and always knew exactly where to position ourselves on the pitch to get the best out of each other.

Alan Mullery and Terry Venables took over in midfield but I never felt really content and comfortable playing with either of them. Both were given a tough time by the Spurs supporters, who had been spoiled over the years and unkindly kept comparing Mullery and Venables with their great idols, Blanchflower and Mackay. It doesn't surprise me that both Alan and Terry have since emerged as promising young managers. Both were always keen students of the game and, although neither of them actually said anything to me, I sensed they would have liked me to have been more conventional and conformist in my approach to football. I liked them both and thought they talked a lot of sense about the game but I've always closed my ears to too much tactical theory. I think a lot of the individual flair and freedom of expression has been coached out of today's players and I was determined not to let anybody stifle my game. I liked to do things *my* way.

Eddie Baily, a lovely bloke with great Cockney humour and a sergeant major voice, tried desperately hard to get through to me with coaching theories but I successfully resisted all approaches. He was a great one for bullying us through our pre-season training runs, nagging us into making greater efforts on long cross-country treks. I could never see the sense in running anywhere without a ball and was always one of the back-markers. I never considered myself a budding Emil Zatopek. Dear old Eddie used to trail us on his bicycle, hurling verbal insults at us in an effort to get us to raise our pace. Once we hid behind a bush and ambushed him and tossed his bike into a canal. He got his own back by making us work even harder in training.

The maddest moment I recall at Tottenham was when Bill Nick and Eddie made us play a twenty-minute practice match without a ball. I remember saying to Cliffie Jones: 'Are we pissed or are they...?'

Things were still 'super' on the social side at Spurs. Alan

Gilzean was a formidable replacement for Bobby Smith both on the pitch and in our drinking school. He and I quickly hit it off as playing partners and I also found him a more than willing partner at the bar. His favourite tipple was Bacardi and coke and he got in so much practice that I would confidently have backed him against *almost* anybody in a drinking contest.

Phil Beal, Jimmy Robertson, Joe Kinnear, Cyril Knowles and occasionally Mike England and Terry Venables joined our Bell and Hare Club where Dave Mackay was still the king. When he moved on to Derby to carry on the legend of the great Mackay, I began to concentrate more on the Essex area for my drinking sessions. I was now dividing my time three ways: between football, my business interests and my drinking.

Bill Nick gave me a quiet, fatherly word of warning about my drinking that went unheeded after a riotous night in Yugoslavia. We had just beaten Hajduk Split in a European Cup Winners' Cup tie and let off steam in a nightclub attached to our hotel.

The Press boys had done some reconnaissance work and told everybody in the Spurs party that there was a sight not to be missed in the nightclub. Even Bill Nick, the last person you would normally expect to find frequenting such places, was intrigued enough to attend the evening's cabaret performance that featured a lady with a 58-inch bust doing an incredible striptease act that involved climbing a rope and removing a tiger skin.

I had shifted about ten pints of beer and was just about to call it a night when two Russians who had seen me play that day invited me to their table where they were drinking a vicious Yugoslav drink called slivovich. They insisted that we should toast the Queen of England and naturally I replied with a toast to the President of the USSR. Over a period of about an hour we must have drunk ten toasts to such diverse characters as the Right Hon. Harold Wilson, Fidel Castro of Cuba, the great Russian goalkeeper Lev Yashin and, would

you believe, Sir Alf Ramsey. By the time I proposed Alf's toast
it came out something like 'Shuralfshramshy ...' I was wide-
eyed and legless when the toasting was finished. Before being
carried to bed I believe I managed to push one of the players
into an indoor swimming pool.

During the flight home the next day, Bill Nick told me
quietly that I was old enough to know better and that he hoped
in future I would not make a public exhibition of myself. He
also suggested that I should cut down on my drinking.

But I didn't listen. I was having too good a time.

5

Drinking for England

'Tis your country bids!
Gloriously drunk, obey th' important call!
– William Cowper (1731–1800)

Dear old Alf Ramsey – Sir Alfred the Great – saw through me in five minutes flat. He was a shrewd judge of people who quickly had me weighed up as a carefree, non-conformist character whose thinking on football was completely the opposite of his cautious, methodical, well-organised approach to the game.

He knew me for what I was from the moment of our very first conversation outside the boundaries of football. It took place just before one of Alf's early games in charge of the England team against Czechoslovakia in Bratislava. Alf was giving us the after-match agenda ... 'The coach will be ready to leave forty-five minutes after the game and we shall go back to the hotel *together*,' he said with that unblinking stare of his that gives listeners the feeling they are being hypnotised.

There was an uneasy shuffling of feet and I could sense that my drinking pals in the England squad were waiting for me to act as their spokesman.

'A few of us were wondering, Alf,' I said, 'whether we could nip out for a couple of drinks before going back to the hotel ... ?'

Now I am going to quote Alf's reply verbatim because, as I was to discover over the years, he only swore when he wanted

to make himself perfectly understood: 'If you want a f------
beer you come back to the hotel and have it ...'

He had made himself perfectly understood!

It wasn't said in a nasty way and there was a hint of a twinkle
in those cold blue eyes of his as they fastened on to me from
beneath rich, thick eyebrows. Alf was just letting us know that
he was in charge. From that moment on, Alf had me marked
down in his photographic memory as a ringleader of the drinking squad.

I scored two goals in a 4–2 win over Czechoslovakia to give
Alf a great start to his first tour as England manager. As I
remember, he bought one of the early rounds when we got
back to the hotel *together*. Downstairs in the hotel we found
a nightclub and the entire squad had a good celebration drink.
Flying to East Germany the next day, several of the hung-over
officials as well as some players were distinctly unwell during
a bumpy flight that helped confirm my belief that man is not
made to fly.

Contrary to what a lot of people think, Alf and I got on
quite well with each other even though we were opposites in
our attitudes about football. He could shift a drink or two
when he wanted and I have had several long sessions with him
after matches when he has let himself go and really given the
gin and tonics a good hiding. When he dropped his mask, he
was a different person altogether to the sombre, unsmiling
man the public knew. He had a nice sense of humour and a
lot of warmth and charm. There were times when I stretched
his charm to breaking point.

We had a good drinking school in that England squad. My
long-time pal Bobby Moore was the man I always roomed with.
I would have to put him pretty high in the table of international drinkers but it didn't stop him being just about the
greatest defender English football has ever produced. There
has never been anybody in the world to touch Mooro for con-
sistency and constant high-performance output. And there are
not many footballers who could match him in a drinking contest. Mooro's got hollow legs and after top-pressure matches

could go through pints of lager without showing any effect from the booze whatsoever. He was in no way a drunkard but enjoyed winding down with a glass in his hand after the match-action was over.

Our liking for a good bevvy got Bobby and me into several scrapes together long before the infamous Blackpool Affair at West Ham. It reached the point where it was rumoured that Alf was ready to relieve Mooro of the England captaincy before the 1966 World Cup triumph. The first time we upset Alf was on the eve of England's departure for a match against Portugal in Lisbon in May 1964. Bobby and I called for volunteers for an evening stroll into London's West End from the Lancaster Gate Hotel where we were staying. With 'elbow men' like Mooro, Greavesie and 'Budgie' Byrne leading the outing it was odds on the stroll becoming something of a stagger before the night was through. In tow along with Budgie we had Gordon Banks, Bobby Charlton, George Eastham and Ray Wilson. We stopped off at a favourite drinking oasis called The Beachcomber and it was fairly late – close to midnight – when we got back to the hotel. Each of us realised our absence-without-leave had been noticed when we found our passports lying on our beds.

This was Alf's stunning but subtle way of letting us know he was not pleased. He left it until the eve of the match four days later before mentioning our little escapade. After our final training session he said: 'You can all go and get changed now apart from the seven players who I believe would like to stay and see me.'

Sheepishly, we stood gathered around Alf while the rest of the squad went back to the dressing-room with quizzical looks over their shoulders. Alf was short, sharp and to the point: 'You are all lucky to be here. If there had been enough players in the squad, I would have left you behind in London. All I hope is that you have learned your lesson and will not do anything silly again ...'

Alf named all seven of us in the England team and we repaid him by beating Portugal 4–3 in an epic match. Two of the

AWOL men – Budgie Byrne and Bobby Charlton – scored the goals, Budgie helping himself to the sweetest of hat-tricks. Alf allowed himself quite a few G-and-Ts that night.

Less than two weeks later Mooro and I were in Alf's bad books again. This time it wasn't booze but music that got us into trouble. We are both Ella Fitzgerald fans and slipped out of our New York hotel on the eve of the match against the United States to catch the 'First Lady' in concert. Neither Bobby nor I were playing against the States (who were hammered 10–0) and we saw no harm in taking a night off. Alf didn't say very much but there was a coldness in his manner at breakfast the next morning that left us in no doubt that he was displeased.

Our next stop was Rio de Janeiro for a match against Brazil and, boy, did we have a hectic time there. We stayed nine days for an international tournament and we worked and played hard both on and off the pitch.

Budgie Byrne, the incredible character who I think I would have to put top of the international drinkers league table, was the life and soul of the party. He was full of funny tricks, such as pushing me fully-clothed in my new England suit into the deep end of the hotel swimming pool. Budgie then had to dive in to pull me out. It was a frightening experience that convinced me I should learn to swim. Ironically the next day Budgie, a strong swimmer, nearly drowned off the Copacabana beach when he got trapped in rough water. Somehow he managed to get ashore but not before going through a nightmare that almost sobered him up!

The football tournament got our full concentration and effort. We were holding Brazil to a 1–1 draw with just twenty minutes to go when Pele hit one of his purple patches and lifted them to a flattering 5–1 victory. This really choked us. Alf knew how we felt and, with four days before the next match, let us off the leash for the night.

At dawn the next morning a team of seven dishevelled-looking England footballers were beaten about 10–0 in an impromptu match by a side of a dozen Copacabana beach boys whose skills were out of this world. The result, thank goodness, never got into the record books.

We flew up to São Paulo from Rio to watch the second match of the mini-World Cup between Brazil and Argentina and I can honestly say I have never witnessed scenes like it. Because there were no seats left in the stand, the entire England party – including players, journalists and officials – were assigned to touchline benches that were just two yards from the pitch and eight or so yards from the fenced-in capacity crowd. It was far too close for comfort.

As soon as we sat down the spectators spotted us and set up a deafening chant of *'Cinco–Uma!'* – Portuguese for five-one – and a derisive reminder of our defeat in Rio. Budgie Byrne couldn't resist the bait and stood up on the bench and started conducting the fans like the man in the white suit before a Wembley Cup Final. The Brazilians loved it and started chanting in time to Budgie's waving arms.

Budgie's choir switched their attention to cheering the Brazilian team when they came out on to the pitch and lit up the night sky by firing dozens of three-stage firework rockets high above the stadium. Then we had fireworks of a different kind on the pitch.

Right from the first whistle Argentinian defender Messiano made it clear that his one intention was to stop Pele from playing. He kicked him, tripped him, spat at him, wrestled him to the floor and pulled his shirt anytime he seemed likely to get past him. Finally, after about thirty minutes of this almost criminal assault, Pele completely lost his temper. He took a running jump at Messiano and butted him full in the face.

The Argentinian was carried off with a broken nose and, incredibly, the Swiss referee let Pele play on!

The calculated, cynical fouling by the Argentinians had knocked all the rhythm and style out of the Brazilians and the stadium became as quiet as a morgue when two minutes from the end the player substituting for the injured Messiano scored his second goal of the match to make it 3–0 to Argentina.

Budgie Byrne unwisely chose this moment to do an insane thing. He stood on the bench again to face the fans and, holding up three fingers, invited them to join him in a chant of 'Three–Zero ...' It was the worst joke of Budgie's life. Suddenly bricks and fireworks rained down from the terraces as the fans turned their disappointment on us. They would have much preferred to have reached the hated Argentinians but we were nearer targets.

The usually impassive Alf Ramsey took one look at the avalanche of bricks, fireworks and rubbish coming our way and gave the shortest tactical talk of his life: 'Run for it, lads ...' Luckily the final whistle had just blown and we made a mad dash for the centre-circle. We later awarded Brian James, of the *Daily Mail*, an imaginary gold medal for being first to the halfway line despite starting at least five yards behind all us players. Frank McGhee of the *Daily Mirror* was voted an award for bravery for sitting it out at the touchline desk where he was writing his report but was later big enough to admit that the only reason he stayed in the firing line was because he had his foot trapped in the struts of the desk.

Frank glared through his glasses in the direction of Budgie and said: 'I felt like a bleedin' scorpion. I'd made up my mind that before I killed myself I would have throttled that mad bastard Byrne. He could have got us all killed ...'

It was Budgie's quick wits that finally got us off the pitch in one piece. As the fans began to scream blue murder despite the intimidating presence of dozens of armed police, Budgie shouted the wise instruction: 'Grab yourself a Brazilian player.'

He then seized goalkeeper Gilmar lovingly by the arm and walked with him off the pitch, knowing full well that no fans would try to harm one of their idols. We all followed Budgie's lead and went off arm-in-arm with bewildered Brazilian players.

You may think that we were over-reacting but uppermost in the minds of everybody in that stadium was the fact that just ten days earlier 301 people had been killed in a riot at the national stadium in Peru where Argentina had been the opponents.

I think the way Argentina had played against Brazil that night – brutally and coldly vicious – stayed imprinted on Alf Ramsey's mind and was one of the reasons he made his 'animals' outburst against them during the 1966 World Cup.

The 1966 World Cup. It seems a lifetime ago ...

Seven months before the 1966 tournament in England I went down with hepatitis, an illness that affects the liver but was not brought on by anything to do with my boozing. It drained me dry of energy and strength. I was out of the game for fifteen weeks and by the time I returned in the February Alf was well ahead with his team-building programme.

I have never worked harder in my life to recapture fitness, even cutting right back on my drinking. This was a time in my life when I could control myself. I was desperately keen to play in the Finals because I was convinced England were going to win. Everything was right for us. We had a great pool of players, vital home advantage and the right mood running through the game at League level. No disrespect to Alf, but I reckoned England would win no matter who was in charge.

That damned hepatitis attack robbed me of a vital half yard of pace but I still believed I was good enough and sharp enough to represent England better than any other striker around. That may sound conceited but any goal scorer who lacks confidence and belief in his own ability is in trouble. I believed in myself and I know that Alf thought I was the right man for the job.

Both Mooro and I clinched our places in the World Cup team during the tour leading up to the finals. Alf toyed with the idea of putting Norman Hunter in the no. 6 shirt but Bobby produced a succession of regally impressive performances that convinced Ramsey that he should retain the West Ham skipper. That decision more than any other won the World Cup for England because Bobby emerged as the player of the tournament, never putting a foot wrong.

I was beginning to motor with some of my old enthusiasm and snap and a goal against Yugoslavia and four against Norway persuaded Alf that I should be in the attack for the opening World Cup match against Uruguay.

We were on a hiding to nothing against Uruguay because everybody expected us to win and anything less than victory meant a lot of stick for England. Uruguay were interested only in stopping us from scoring and packed their penalty area with nine defenders. It was an undistinguished start but even after the goalless draw I still knew in my heart that England were going to win the World Cup. What I didn't know is that they were going to do it without me.

Alf made two changes for the second match against Mexico, replacing Alan Ball and John Connolly with Terry Paine and Martin Peters. Ballie, another of my drinking partners, was sick with Alf and talked about going home. But over a lager we helped him see the sense of staying on and he played a prominent part in England's victory against West Germany in the Final.

We began to find our momentum against Mexico. I did not score but felt satisfied with my contribution towards England's 2–0 win. I missed a couple of chances against France in the third match but we beat them comfortably 2–0. After the game I had four stitches inserted in a gash on my shin. It was an injury that provided the excuse for my exit from the tournament.

Alf quite properly preferred a 100 per cent fit player for the quarter-final against Argentina and Geoff Hurst took my place for his World Cup debut. He gladly grabbed the opportunity and headed a fine goal from a perfect Martin Peters pass to give England a 1–0 victory.

Argentina were less violent but just as niggling as they had been against Brazil in São Paulo and their captain Rattin, a gifted but temperamental player, was sent off for trying to referee the match. I agreed with Alf's uncharacteristic outburst afterwards when he described the Argentinians as 'animals'. I was delighted to see that by the time they came to stage the 1978 World Cup they had tamed their tempers and flourished only their great talents.

The semi-final against Portugal was the classic the match with Argentina could have been. I was still nursing the injury, which was practically healed, and watched from the touchline as Bobby Charlton majestically conducted England's well-deserved 2–1 victory.

At the end of the semi-final I felt in my bones that Alf was not going to select me for the Final. My dream of helping England win the World Cup was about to be smashed. I was fit for selection and the Press boys began churning out, 'Greaves must play' or 'Greaves must not play' stories – according to how *they* saw it. But only one bloke knew for sure whether I was going to make it. Alf Ramsey. And he wasn't saying a dickie bird.

The Saturday of the Final came and still I did not know for sure whether I was in or out. But I sensed that Alf was being a little distant and guessed he had made up his mind to pick an unchanged team. I knew for certain at mid-day and I had guessed right.

In fact I had been so sure that on the morning of the match, my room-mate Bobby Moore had woken up to find me packing my bags. 'What are you doing Jim?' he queried, sitting up in bed at the start of what was to be the greatest day in his life.

'Just getting ready for a quick getaway once the match is over,' I told him.

'You can do that tomorrow morning,' he said. 'We'll all be on the bevvy tonight. Celebrating our World Cup win.'

Alf didn't say much to me. Just said he had decided on an unchanged team and thought I would understand. 'Sure, Alf,' I told him. 'They'll win it for you.'

'I think so,' he said, and then was gone to talk to other players who had been left out.

People have often asked me since what Alf had to say to me when he told me I was out of the side. What could he say? He knew I was choked but he was doing what he believed to

57

be right. There were ten other blokes in the squad as unlucky as me so there was no reason why Alf had to sort me out for a special word of sympathy. Not that I was seeking anybody's sympathy. I felt sorry for myself and sick that I was out. But I was not and never have been in any way bitter against Alf. He did his job and England won the World Cup.

It says a lot for the wonderful team spirit that Alf had built up that all eleven of the players who had been left out swallowed their self pity and gave their total support to the eleven players who were representing us against West Germany. We were out there on the pitch with them in spirit and I felt as exhausted as if I had played after the game had gone into extratime. Geoff Hurst went on to complete his now historic hattrick to clinch a 4–2 victory and, of course, the championship.

I danced around the pitch with everybody else but even in this great moment of triumph I felt a sickness in my stomach that I had not taken part in the match of a lifetime. It was my saddest day in football.

As the celebrations got into full swing I quietly returned to the hotel, picked up my bags and slipped off home. I was told later by Mooro that Alf thought I had deliberately snubbed him after the game but that is far from the truth. I was delighted for Alf and didn't want to spoil his moment of glory by letting him see the hurt in my eyes.

I went home and quietly got drunk. Late that night I went off on a family holiday. The 1966 World Cup was suddenly history.

In my time as an England player there was one team better than the side that won the World Cup in 1966. This was the side of the Walter Winterbottom era that in a winning sequence of five matches scored thirty-two goals and conceded only eight.

The high spot was when we slammed a Scotland side including Dave Mackay, Denis Law and Ian St John 9–3 at Wembley in 1961. I scored a hat-trick and Bobby Smith and Johnny Haynes got two goals each.

That team still runs easily off my tongue: Ron Springett, Jimmy Armfield, Mick McNeil, Bobby Robson, Peter Swan, Ron Flowers, Bryan Douglas, myself, Bobby Smith, Johnny Haynes, Bobby Charlton.

If you could have grafted that attack into a team containing the 1966 England defence, you would have had the greatest England international side of all time.

Unfortunately that 1961 team came to the boil too early. We were past our peak by the time the 1962 World Cup came round and we were eliminated after struggling through to the quarter-finals. Had the tournament been staged twelve months earlier, I am convinced England would have at least reached the Final.

I played just three more times for England after the 1966 World Cup. Then after about a year out of the international picture I suddenly started pumping in goals for Spurs in something like my old style. There was quite a campaign in the Press for my reinstatement and Alf – now, Sir Alf – was moved to say: 'I am being crucified because I am not selecting Greaves, yet he has told me that he does not want to play for England.'

I was astonished by that statement because deep down I still wanted to play for my country and, despite what some people may have thought, was always passionately proud to wear the white shirt of England. Early in my career I was the victim of a damaging misquote. It was claimed that I had said that I 'had no fire in my belly' when playing for England. I never uttered those words but they appeared in print and many people took them as gospel and thought I played with less than total commitment when on international duty. I promise you I always gave my best for England and can point to forty-four goals in fifty-seven matches as evidence.

Alf completely misunderstood me if he really did believe that I had asked him not to select me to play for England anymore. What I had said to Alf during my last training session with his squad at Roehampton was that I would rather not be called up unless I was going to play.

At the time, Alf had got into the habit of including me in

his training squad and then not naming me to play in the match. He told me it was useful to have a player of my experience on the sidelines. All it did was frustrate me and as quite an active businessman in those days I knew there were plenty of things I could be doing rather than continually waste hours at training get-togethers which, for me, had no end product.

Let's face it, I was never the most enthusiastic of trainers. I'm the bloke who used to steal rides on milk floats and farm tractors during cross country runs at Tottenham. And it was me who found the only drinking place within walking distance of Lilleshall, that fitness fanatics' paradise.

It is in the middle of nowhere, a grand manor that has been transformed into a magnificent training centre for all sportsmen. Maybe it is a great place for the muscles but I didn't find it too clever for the mind or the throat. Lilleshall is as dry as a desert! This of course delighted the likes of Alf Ramsey and his faithful right hand man Harold Shepherdson who were relieved to have their squad of players closeted together away from all distracting temptations. But they reckoned without the cunning mind of a drinker like me.

One evening somebody mentioned the possibility of playing golf the next day. Golf! To me that meant one thing. A clubhouse. I talked Mooro and a couple of the other lads into joining me for an evening constitutional. I led them across country to the golf course and there it was in full swing – the clubhouse bar.

Harold Shep, a smashing bloke who was physiotherapist, baggageman and general handyman to the England team for more than 150 international matches, used to have the job of making sure all players were safely tucked up in bed at a reasonable hour. I remember one time when we stayed in the 1900-room Waldorf Astoria in New York when that job got almost too much for him but at an out-of-the-way place like Lilleshall he expected no problems.

We had been bevvying in the golf clubhouse for a couple of hours when Shep walked in on us. 'Got you!' he said in triumph. He looked at me, unable to keep the grin off his face. 'You,' he said, 'would manage to find a bar in the middle of the Sahara ...'

When I think of Harold Shep I always remember my first international match for England against Peru back in 1959. Well, not the match so much as the nightmare flight we had to get to Lima where the game was played.

Shep knew I was a nervous – paranoic even – flier and sat with me on the flight from Rio de Janeiro to Lima and did his best to take my mind off the fact that we were off the ground. Anybody who ever saw my attempts at heading a ball will know I am happiest with my feet firmly on the floor. As Shep was talking I just happened to look out of the plane window and nearly died of shock. We were flying below the peaks of the Andes and were so low you could actually see the pack horses on the high passes bringing the copper ore out of the mountains.

Just then John Camkin, who was then a journalist with the *News Chronicle*, came walking casually down the aisle from the direction of the pilot's cabin. John had been a bomber crew navigator during the war and flying to him was just like taking a bus ride down the High Street. He stopped by Shep and said very casually: 'I've just been talking to the captain of this old ship. He tells me he normally takes the short route over the top of the Andes but because of the BBC's heavy camera equipment he has decided to fly through the Southern Pass which will make the trip a bit longer.'

It took several seconds for this travelogue to sink in and then I leaned across Shep and said: 'Excuse me Wing Commander Camkin. Can you please go to the flight deck and tell Captain Biggles that the VIP passengers on board have had a vote and they have decided that the best thing he can do is chuck the f------ cameras overboard and fly a little higher ...!'

Old Shep fell about laughing. But I was too scared to raise a smile.

The next day I played my first game for England and scored

our goal in a dismal 4–1 defeat. Nine years later Alf Ramsey decided I no longer figured in his plans.

I wasn't complaining. I had loved every minute of my England career. The goals and the pints ...

6

Counting the mistakes

But I'm not so think as you drunk I am.
– Sir John Squire (1884–1958)

Now that I can look back and see everything in focus without studying life through the bottom of a glass, I can clearly discern where and when I made my biggest mistakes ...

I agreed to leave Tottenham;
I cocked a deaf ear to approaches from Brian Clough;
I agreed to join West Ham.

Later came the biggest mistake of them all. I decided to quit League football. From then on I was hurrying down the finishing straight to a life as an alcoholic.

Bill Nicholson had dropped me for the first time in my career at Tottenham following an FA Cup defeat at Crystal Palace. For several weeks my career just came to a standstill and I spent more time on motor rally trial runs than I did on football matters. I had accepted an offer from the Ford Motor Company to join their team for the 1970 *Daily Mirror* sponsored World Cup rally to Mexico and my co-driver, Tony Fall, was giving me a crash course – not literally of course – in rally driving.

I took the rally so seriously that Bill Nick read it as a sign that I was losing my appetite for football. Maybe he was right at the time but it would quickly have been rekindled with the encouragement of a recall to the first team. Once Nick had made up his mind to drop me I became an embarrassment to him. It was none of my doing but everytime he selected a team without my name in it the Press pestered him. Finally I got fed up with hanging about and asked Bill about my future.

We both considered whether the best thing for all concerned would be for me to move. Both of us were reluctant to commit ourselves to making the break. I looked upon Tottenham as a second home and Bill Nick was only too aware that in just the previous season I had been the club's top goalscorer for the umpteenth time. He knew I would not settle for the indignity and frustration of continually playing in the reserves. He agreed to think about letting me go but nothing definite was decided.

It quickly got around on the football grapevine that I could be on the move and Brian Clough, then manager of Derby County, let me know through a third party that he would be very interested in signing me. My big regret now is that I did not bother to contact him.

Cloughie and I played together in two England international matches back in 1959 before a knee injury tragically ended his career. Even then he was a cocky, confident character with loads of belief in his own ability. It wasn't misplaced confidence because he could certainly play a bit although he struggled to establish himself in the England attack. At that time Joe Baker and Bobby Smith were both challenging for the no. 9 shirt and the selectors, prematurely in my opinion, tossed him out after a 1–1 draw with Wales and a 3–2 defeat by Sweden.

Now, ten years later, he was back in my life as one of the most dynamic and successful young managers in the game. He had revitalised Dave Mackay's career by taking him to Derby and my old drinking pal was full of good reasons why I should follow him up the motorway to the Baseball Ground. But I had my mind full of the rally and my businesses were beginning to build up and at the time Derby seemed to be a million miles away. Yet now I appreciate that Cloughie would have been just the man to get hold of me and motivate me into producing something of my old form.

There is no question that he has got an aura about him that brings out the best in the people around and about him. In all honesty, I think he should have been given the job of England manager ahead of Ron Greenwood.

I am sure Ron, a man of great intelligence and deep knowledge of world football, will do a sound job but he lacks the motivating powers of Cloughie. Ron talks a lovely game of football but he has not got that Clough magic of being able to make players ready to run through walls for him. One of the major mistakes of my career was not giving Cloughie the chance to switch me back on.

On transfer deadline day – 16 March 1970 – I was busily settling the family into a new house when I got a telephone call from Bill Nick. He said Martin Peters was at White Hart Lane with him and had agreed to sign for Spurs. Ron Greenwood was waiting at Upton Park to talk to me.

Looking back on that day, I wish to God I had told Bill that I was not interested. He would still have completed the signing of Martin from West Ham because the £54,000 valuation put on me as a makeweight in the deal was chickenfeed to Spurs. But I had been so switched off from football that I was not thinking straight and agreed to go and see Greenwood. It seemed such a convenient move at the time.

I knew I could have done a lot better financially because I'd had several very tasty offers made on the old hush-hush while I was out of the Tottenham team. Those people who seem to think that I made a fortune out of football may be interested and perhaps surprised to learn that never throughout my career did I earn a basic wage of more than £100 a week. I was receiving nothing illegal or mind-boggling from West Ham but the thought of joining Mooro and Geoff Hurst and the fact that the Hammers training ground was just a fifteen-minute drive from my home and businesses lulled me into a signing that I have regretted ever since.

In a way I did not do myself any favours at West Ham by banging in two goals in my debut at Manchester City, one of the clubs that had been interested in signing me. I set myself a standard that I could not maintain. We scrambled out of relegation trouble at the death of that season and then I gave all my concentration to the World Cup rally. The last – and worst – season of my League career was a matter of three months away.

But before that I had to go through hell on four wheels.

If anybody asked me what was the toughest thing I have had to do in life – apart from trying to give up drink – I would say without hesitation: 'Driving in the 1970 World Cup rally.'

How I survived in one piece I will never know. Only twenty-three of the ninety-six starters from Wembley Stadium finished the 16,245 mile race and I am proud to say I was one of them. Thanks mainly to the brilliant driving of my co-driver Tony Fall, we finished sixth in our black-and-white Ford Escort that I thought several times during the marathon was going to become our hearse.

We used to go fifty-five hours in one stretch without sleep as we navigated the toughest terrain in the world, driving at speeds of up to 100 mph. on mountain roads that were built with only donkey transport in mind. I conscientiously followed the rule of the road 'Don't Drink and Drive' and the only alcohol I consumed during the rally was while we were on the flight across to Rio after we had tackled the mountains of Serbia in the European half of the event.

Mind you, there were plenty of terrifying times when I wanted to turn to the bottle for comfort.

Seventy-one cars left Rio for speed tests which took place during tropical floods which made driving treacherous and dangerous. We sped through clouds of red dust and then suddenly through flooded roads and along miles of cramped, bumpy roads. It was such a tough stage of the rally that at the end of it only fifty-two cars were left. Next we faced the

Argentine pampas, the gaucho country. We had to maintain an average speed of sixty mph for twenty-four hours which was made all the harder because the rarified air reduced engine power by almost half. We were 15,000 feet up into the Andes on a narrow winding mountain road when we lost a rear wheel. We had already used our spare and we finished that stage with me at the wheel and Tony at the back pushing.

We lost a wheel again on the next stage but it could so easily have been our lives. Tony was driving and I was navigating as we came down a steep and narrow mountain road. Suddenly an old peasant woman crossed in front of us. Miraculously Tony swerved the car past her and skidded to a stop on the mountain edge as a wheel axle broke. We were literally feet away from death and I hardly dared breathe as my brilliant co-driver carefully manouevred the car back into the centre of the road before we jacked it up and started urgent repairs. In all we suffered eleven punctures, a damaged suspension and a broken half shaft. But we got our battered vehicle through to the finish in Mexico after witnessing the aftermath of a terrible earthquake in Lima and landslides in Ecuador.

At the end of it all I made up for lost drinking time and recall jumping fully clothed into a swimming pool – I had learned to swim by then – and sitting paralytic drunk in an armchair that had been thrown into the pool. If I had realised how hard the race was going to be I doubt if I could have summoned up the courage to face it. Those rally drivers are among the toughest and most fearless sportsmen I have ever met. There were times when I felt physically sick over the demands of the race and several times wanted to quit but there was no way I could let Tony Fall down. One frightening incident stands out in my mind like a nightmare. We were speeding along a winding road deep in the heart of Panama. It was pitch-black and Tony was at the wheel. I was trying to fall asleep when suddenly I felt the car swerving. We were travelling at about 100 mph and right ahead of us was a horse galloping at full speed. Tony couldn't possibly avoid it. He tried, using every bit of his enormous driving skill but we collided head on. The poor horse's head was ripped clean off and its hooves smashed through our windscreen as it bounced against the bonnet of the car. Tony and I were splattered with blood and glass and shaking like leaves in a wind. We both felt sick for hours afterwards and became very depressed. But we had to force ourselves out of the mood to concentrate on the road ahead.

Thankfully for the sake of our sanity there were also a lot of laughs along the way. I remember one breakdown in Chile when we seemed to be in the middle of nowhere. I went looking for help and thumbed down a bus that was going, so I thought, to the garage that we had left behind. About an hour later I was walking back to Tony with my hands buried in my pockets and my head bowed to hide a sheepish smile. The bus had taken me in the opposite direction to what I wanted. Shows you what a good navigator I was! With a map in my hand I wasn't bad but when it came to bus routes in Chile I was useless.

We arrived in Mexico City just twenty-four hours after Bobby Moore had flown in from Bogota after his infamous arrest on a trumped-up jewel theft charge. Bobby had been hidden away from the world's Press in an embassy house on the outskirts of the city. I knew Mooro would welcome the company of some old drinking pals after his harrowing experience and so with big Lou Wade in tow I booked a cab – I was finished with driving for the next month or so – and went to visit the England captain. When we arrived at the house it was under siege from an army of journalists and TV cameramen. I sought out the BBC's man on the spot, David Coleman, and asked him what was going on. David said nobody was being allowed in. But I decided to slip quietly in the back way and told Lou to cause a diversion at the front. This was quite simple for Lou because all he had to do was parade in front of the cameras to be guaranteed everybody's attention. Lou, a football fanatic and one of Mooro's business associates back home in Essex, is six foot seven inches tall and, to say the least, fairly loud in his mode of dress. This particular evening as I recall he was wearing bright red trousers, a yellow and green checked jacket, a frilly yellow shirt and a wide, dazzling tie. All eyes were on this technicolor spectacle as I nipped past the guards and climbed over the rear garden wall. I got into the back of the house through some French windows and Mooro almost dropped his lager in surprise when he saw me approaching from the direction of the kitchen. The wife of the embassy official was furious and ordered me out, insisting that I go through the pantomime of ringing the doorbell before she would officially admit me. Outside the TV cameras whirred and bewildered journalists looked on open-mouthed as I came sheepishly out of the front door only to be let back in one minute later, this time with the incredible Lou Wade as company. I think the embassy official's wife was close to fainting when she caught sight of Lou!

The first thing I asked Mooro is what he had done with the bracelet he was supposed to have stolen. That set the tone for the evening and we raided the embassy cocktail cabinet and had a good relaxing drink. Mooro and I were just practising for the many long sessions we had together at West Ham. One night out in Blackpool got us on to the front pages of all the national newspapers and made me lose a lot of respect for Ron Greenwood.

For somebody with what was slowly but surely becoming a drink problem, I could not have gone to a worse club than West Ham. They had a drinking school there that could have taken on the old Bell and Hare crew of Tottenham and possibly drunk them under the table. It would have been a close match and would no doubt have gone into extra-time.

The regulars in the Hammers school were Mooro – like Mackay, the king of the barstool – John Cushley, Brian Dear, Frank Lampard, John Charles, Harry Redknapp, Jimmy Lindsay and, occasionally, Geoff Hurst. I was quickly accepted into the school. I not only prided myself on my drinking capacity but also on always paying my way. The difference between that West Ham team and the Spurs players I had left behind was that Tottenham could really turn it on where it mattered on the pitch. I found that with the obvious few exceptions like Mooro, Hurstie and Billy Bonds, West Ham was heavily populated with mediocre players. That may sound tough but it is fact. And I must be honest and admit that in my time at West Ham I could be placed in the mediocre bracket. They have little to thank me for apart from a handful of goals that helped save them from a relegation that at one stage in the season looked a certainty.

I had always promised myself that the moment I stopped enjoying my football I would quickly hang up my boots. And from the start of that 1970–1 season with West Ham I was thoroughly miserable about West Ham's game and my contribution to it. Even as early as the September of the season I had seriously considered packing it in. That was after a terrible 4–1 defeat at Newcastle. Ron Greenwood told Mooro and me that he was considering resigning and my reaction was that if he went I would go as well.

Mind you, the circumstances in which Ron made his confession were strange to say the least. We were in the upstairs bar of a Jumbo jet on the way to New York at the time. West Ham were to play Santos – plus Pele – in an exhibition match in New York. It was laughable really after the exhibition we had made of ourselves at Newcastle two days earlier.

Anyway, Mooro and I plus a business pal of his, Freddie Harrison, were getting stuck into the golden liquid at the bar, when Ron Greenwood joined us from downstairs and requested a Coke. It was none of my doing but I must admit having a juvenile giggle when I noticed Freddie lacing the Coke with Bacardi. During the next hour Ron must have had about another five or six Cokes, all of them doctored by the mischievous Freddie. It was a diabolical thing to do and I shouldn't think Ron ever forgave Mooro and I for it, although we were only onlookers.

Ron finally realised what was going on and to his credit laughed it off. The alcohol made his tongue much looser than he would have liked and he confessed that he was thinking of resigning. I felt choked in a way because here was a man who had always done his honest, level best for West Ham and had made them into a club renowned throughout Europe for the quality of their football. But he had recently lost his way and I had done absolutely nothing to help him get back on the right path.

He returned to his seat where he went into a heavy, drink-sedated sleep. Peter Eustace, a comical Yorkshireman who was not exactly Ron's number one fan, had the rest of the West Ham party in fits of laughter as he leant over the snoring figure of Greenwood, miming as if he was telling him exactly what he thought of him. I think Ron would have had a fit if he had woken up.

As the Jumbo prepared to touch down in New York, I vowed that if Greenwood quit I would get out of the game for good. But he never mentioned resigning again and I stayed until the end of that miserable season.

I made up my mind to retire after the Blackpool Affair which was blown up out of all proportion by the media. On New Year's Night, Mooro and I were preparing to go to bed after a couple of lagers each in the restaurant of the Imperial Hotel where West Ham were staying on the eve of an FA Cup tie at Blackpool. As we were walking through the hotel lobby we got into conversation with some BBC television cameramen who were in town to film our match. They were waiting for a taxi to take them to ex-boxer Brian London's 007 nightclub. 'There's little chance of the game being played tomorrow,' one of the cameramen said. 'The pitch is iced over. It will be a miracle if it's fit for play. I think we're all wasting our time up here. What a way to start a New Year.'

Then we were interrupted by the hotel doorman calling to the cameramen: 'Your two taxis have arrived.'

'But we only wanted one,' said the BBC man. Completely on impulse, I said: 'Don't worry. We'll take the other one.'

I had set the timebomb ticking. It would be another seventy-two hours or so before it went off. Mooro and I jauntily walked towards the hotel door and collected the thirsty Brian Dear and the casually interested Clyde Best on the way. 'We're just nipping down to Brian London's place for a quick nightcap,' we told them. Dear came along for the drink. Best came along for the ride.

Two hours later – at about 1.45 am. – we were back at the Imperial ordering coffee and sandwiches. It was as stupid and as innocent as that. I was the only one who had really got stuck into the booze – about a dozen lagers, which was par for the course for me at that time. Mooro and Dear had drunk five or six each and Clyde Best had sipped his way through one soft drink.

The next day, after sleeping through until ten in the morning, we went to the Blackpool ground where a skating rink of a pitch had somehow been passed fit. John Curry might have felt at home on it. We then committed the real 'crime'. We lost to Blackpool. We lost not because of that late-night drink ... not because of the state of the pitch ... but simply because we were not good enough. The team lacked understanding and cohesion.

On the Monday a West Ham supporter telephoned the club and a newspaper saying that he had seen us drunk in Brian London's club on the eve of the match. He may have seen us but we were certainly not drunk.

I was sickened and disgusted by the way the West Ham board – in particular Ron Greenwood – handled the situation. They fined us and dropped us and did it in the full glare of publicity. The story was plastered all over the front pages as if we had been guilty of the crime of the century.

We deserved to have disciplinary action taken against us but it could easily have been done privately. I was particularly nauseated by the treatment Bobby Moore got. No player has given more loyal service – and top-quality service, at that – than Bobby did to West Ham.

But just one step out of line and they cut his legs off.

I was now back to using drink as a crutch. Because I was not enjoying my football I was getting into an agitated state but found that once I had got a few drinks inside me my concern and worry drifted away.

In my last few months at West Ham I began to shift beer in bigger quantities than ever. After training at Chadwell Heath I would go to Jack Slater's pub opposite Romford Greyhound Stadium and drink right through until closing time.

Most evenings I would prop up any number of bars near my Upminster home.

Suddenly football didn't matter to me any more. All I was interested in was drinking. Once I had five, six or seven lagers in me I would get a click in my head and the world would seem a rosy place.

You don't need football, Jimbo. Ron Greenwood and West Ham can go and stuff themselves. I'll have just a couple more pints, then I'll go home ...

73

7

Hitting rock bottom

Of seeming arms to make a short essay,
Then hasten to be drunk, the business of the day.
– John Dryden (1631–1700)

I should warn readers of a nervous disposition that we now come to the harrowing part of my story. A lot of it has been pieced together from evidence of eyewitnesses to my drunken downfall. Much of it to me is just a blur on my memory screen. The victim of a road smash is always the one who knows least about it. And that's how it was with me. All I know is that in five years I managed to wreck my life.

When I retired from football at the age of thirty-one I was suddenly like a prisoner let out of jail. I was free of all the discipline of the last sixteen years. No more training. No more do-this-do-that. No more curfews. It was like paradise. Only now, looking back, can I see that it was a fool's paradise. And I was the bloody fool.

For two years after quitting West Ham I didn't touch a football or go near a football ground. In no time at all I put on nearly two stone in weight, a few pounds of it because of lack of exercise but most of it because I was drinking solidly throughout the day, every day. My regular routine was to call in at my businesses for a couple of hours each morning but never stay long enough to risk missing opening time. Throughout most of my football career I had been a beer man but once

I retired I adopted the 'anything goes' approach. By each lunchtime I would have poured several large vodkas down my throat on top of a minimum six pints of beer. Lunchtime was bartime. A couple of Guinnesses, maybe a roll or a pub ploughman and then a pint or two more before closing time. I would then go home and sleep it off in an armchair ready for the evening assault on the bars of Upminster. At the end of the day I would have got through sixteen pints and anything up to eight or so shorts. No trouble.

My wife Irene was appalled by the way I let my physical condition deteriorate. She was the first to realise I had a problem. Me? I was too busy enjoying myself to think of it being a problem. I could stop at any time I wanted to. Or so I thought.

At this stage I was financially secure. The box-and-packaging business I had started up with my brother-in-law, Tom, with a £1000 bank loan on my return from Milan had mushroomed into a small but flourishing empire with a £1 million turnover. Our interests included a country club, sports good shops, a transport firm, insurance and travel agencies and ladies and menswear shops. I was chairman of the parent company and in my sober moments gave all my attention to the businesses. This often involved taking prospective clients out to eat and, of course, to drink. That was my favourite part of the work.

I kept up this pace for two years. And then the *real* drinking started.

The alcoholic is a cunning animal. He can find ways of having drink available twenty-four hours a day. I recall a famous story about Errol Flynn that illustrates my point. He was on strict orders to leave the booze alone after a prolonged drinking bout. The nurse supervising him was content that her patient was behaving himself as he sucked on an orange to satisfy his thirst. What she didn't know was that Flynn had injected vodka into all the oranges on his bedside cabinet with a syringe.

I had never been a great one for boozing at home. In my early drinking days it was the atmosphere of a pub that appealed to me almost as much as the contents of my glass. But once I had got into my drinking stride after leaving West Ham I found there was no way I could go a waking hour without a drink. I started to smuggle bottles of vodka into the house and hide them out of Irene's sight so that she didn't know just how much I was getting down me. She would see me taking the occasional drink from the cocktail cabinet and would grumble that I was drinking too much. When her back was turned I would refill my glass from a bottle craftily hidden in a cupboard in my study or in the wardrobe in our bedroom.

Irene put my drinking down to the fact that I had retired from football too early. Of course, she was right. But I would never admit to a soul that I was missing the game. As long as I had a drink in my hand, I was happy. But out of nowhere I was getting hit by deep depressions and became moody and morose between drinking sessions. Often I would roll home drunk out of my head with no knowledge at all where I had been. During these terrible times I used to put Irene and the kids through hell. All my frustration at knowing what I was doing to myself and not being able to stop used to manifest itself in wild displays of uncontrolled anger. I broke windows, knocked doors off their hinges and occasionally tried to hit Irene. She learned to judge my moods and knew when to keep out of my way. It must have been terrifying for her.

For the next two years I drank heavily *knowing* I had become an alcoholic. This was drinking not just because I wanted to but because I *needed* to. Sometimes during a day I would get through as many as eighteen or twenty pints of beer and then knock back a bottle of vodka at home. I got into the habit of putting a bottle by the side of my bed so that I could have a drink first thing in the morning. This was to stop my hands shaking and to get my engine into working order for the day. Irene and I decided that football could be a cure and I made a comeback of sorts with my local Brentwood team and then with Chelmsford. But it was a half-hearted effort and I gave it up to concentrate full time on drinking. Sometimes I miscalculated or misplaced my reserves of vodka at home and would be on the doorstep of the local supermarket when it opened. I would pick up a wire basket and throw some groceries in as a pretence that I was out shopping for my wife and would then go to the off-licence drinks section and pick up a couple of bottles of vodka, pay for my purchases and hurry home as quickly as possible to get some drink inside me.

The last person who wants to recognise the symptoms of alcoholism is the alcoholic. For two years I did my best to kid myself that drink had not become a problem. I would pack it up after the next session.

Next week, Jimbo, you will go on the wagon. Start getting fit again. Play a bit of squash, some golf and maybe join a Sunday team. Blimey, I'm only thirty-four. I'll pack up drinking and play a lot of sport. Starting next week ...

Of course, next week never came. I did start playing a lot of sport. Golf, squash, tennis and the occasional charity and Sunday matches. But the drinking continued and being physically fit meant I had a faster recovery rate after my heavy sessions than most alcoholics. People would see me competing at sport and never believe that they were watching somebody who within the past forty-eight hours had knocked back two bottles of vodka and a couple of gallons of beer.

They say you are an alcoholic when drinking starts to cost you more than money. I was now well into that league. It was costing me the love of my wife, the respect of my kids and my standing in business. I decided to make my great effort to pull myself together and agreed to go into a private nursing home for treatment and supervision. For a month they gradually reduced my craving for drink and I came out convinced that I had conquered the monster in one go. No chance.

For several weeks I left the booze alone. I didn't need it anymore. As I had always known, I could beat it at anytime that I really put my mind to it. Now I would drink only in moderation. Just a couple of pints a day ...

In no time at all those couple of pints a day had become a couple of gallons a day. Then it was back on the spirits. Then it was back into the nursing home.

This is how I spent the next three years of my life as my world crashed around me. Drinking. Nursing home. Drinking. Nursing home. At least a dozen times I went away for private treatment. I saw a procession of psychiatrists, paid out hundreds of pounds for advice and then ignored it all. I was a helpless alcoholic.

My doctor, a former Olympic competitor who knew all about the pressures and problems of top-line sportsmen suddenly cut off from their mainline activity, put me in touch with Alcoholics Anonymous. I went along to a few of their meetings but was unimpressed.

What a load of waffle they all speak. They are people with a real drink problem. I'll never sink as low as some of them. Now where shall we go for a drink, Jimbo ...?

Now I was at my rock bottom. Irene, who had lovingly nursed me for two years, had reached breaking point and could take no more. I moved in with my parents and used to call in at home just to see the kids.

Tom, my brother-in-law and partner in business, had seen the strain I was putting on Irene, his sister, and this hurt him more than the fact that I was giving less and less attention to the businesses. We started to have our differences and I now accept that I was almost totally to blame for them. Finally, I sold out my interest in the company that Tom and I had so proudly and conscientiously built up over the years. I was left with a couple of menswear shops and a travel agency, which is the worst possible business for an alcoholic to be in because it requires a lot of PR and that meant a ready-made excuse for drinking sessions. The clothes shops went bust, mainly because of the poor economic climate of the time but also due in part to my boozing which had impaired my judgement.

People close to me knew my problem but it was not generally well known in the football world. In my sober moments after nursing home treatment I would show glimpses of my old skill in charity and testimonial matches. Keith Burkinshaw and Bill Nicholson were so impressed by my display for Spurs in a Pat Jennings testimonial match at White Hart Lane that they tried to talk me into making a comeback with Tottenham. They would have been shocked beyond belief had they been able to see the state I was in just a few days earlier at the end of a particularly vicious bender during which I tried to drink Essex dry.

I went as far as discussing the possibility of a return with Spurs with Professional Footballers' Association chairman Derek Dougan but in the end 'swallowed' the idea, not because I didn't want to play League soccer again but because I did not want to let Spurs down. I knew that I was a slave to the bottle and it would not have been fair on the club that I loved to have risked making them look fools.

Spurs had even allowed me to become the first Tottenham player to have a testimonial match at White Hart Lane. On a marvellous night at White Hart Lane, a crowd of 43,000 turned out to see me lead a Spurs team against Feyenoord. This was Tottenham's recognition of my nine years with them. Other stars like Dave Mackay, Cliffie Jones and Bobby Smith had been allowed to leave the club at giveaway transfer fees so that they could negotiate the best possible deal for themselves. I had not been given that opportunity but this memorable testimonial night was more than compensation.

After all expenses had been paid I collected a cheque for £22,000 and I wish to go on record to all those marvellous fans who came to give me their support with the promise that not a penny of the money went on booze. I became a member of Lloyds Underwriters with £12,000 and spent the rest on house improvements.

That beautiful house is now owned by Irene. And well she has earned it. While I was hitting the bottle she fought to hold her world together, for the sake of the kids as much as anything. With me in an alcoholic fog, she got power of attorney over my business affairs and sold out some of my interests to raise enough money to keep the house. Then she borrowed some money to go into a partnership of her own, in a pub of all things. We are now divorced but on speaking terms and we spend family weekends together with our fabulous children.

She has become a State Enrolled Nurse after three years of study and is well adjusted to her new way of life.

Quite a girl, my Irene.

There was no way our marriage could survive the pressures that I put on it. I can remember little of it but I am assured that during my worst drinking bouts I was a pig of a man. I can recall the nightmare of the DTs, lying on my back shaking uncontrollably and having all sorts of terrifying hallucinations. Walls moved and came crashing towards me, inanimate objects became mobile, horrific figures and I could see haunting faces in every corner of the room. I was in hell.

I would stumble around the house with a three-day growth of stubble on my chin, not knowing whether it was night or day. I could no longer afford the luxury of private nursing homes. When I became impossible to handle, friends used to take me to the alcoholic ward of Warley mental hospital. I was in there so many times they must have thought I was a member of the staff.

Incredibly, people still wanted me in football. Dave Underwood, chairman of Barnet, knew about my problem and suggested that football would be the cure. I started to play for Barnet in the Southern League but I was still heavily under the influence.

I was managing to leave drink alone for weeks at a stretch but would then go on almighty benders after which I would invariably end up in Warley hospital. St Antonio Football Club of America wanted me to join them and their representative was given a number where he could contact me. I talked to him for five minutes before convincing him that there was no way I could play for him. Little did he know it but while he was talking to me I was lying flat on my back on a hospital bed hardly able to hold on to the telephone for the shakes.

Inevitably, Fleet Street found out about my problem and I made a public confession. I did not go looking for the publicity but once it was out I decided to use it to my advantage. I knew that with everybody knowing about my illness, I would be on public show and I was hoping that my pride might then help me to defeat the monster.

But I needed help. I turned once more, this time with conviction, to Alcoholics Anonymous.

My name is Jimmy G. I am a professional footballer and I am an alcoholic ...

8

Sober ... just for today

Look to this day, for it is life
The very life of life
– Indian poem

During this chapter you may suspect that I have become almost evangelical about Alcoholics Anonymous. You would be right. I am ready and eager to preach the AA gospel at, for the want of a better phrase, the drop of a drink. When I at last started taking Alcoholics Anonymous seriously, I was a helpless drink addict lost on the road to nowhere. They have saved me from drinking myself to death and have given new shape and meaning to my life.

I now live just one day at a time. This is the AA doctrine. Take twenty-four hours at a time. All I have to do is avoid having a drink today. Just for today.

You never conquer alcoholism. It is a cunning illness that can creep up and hit you when you least suspect it. All AA members, old and new, are constantly reminded to avoid having *one* drink for *one* day and that being sober yesterday is no guarantee of being sober tomorrow. Yesterdays and tomorrows have no more place in my life. I live only for today.

And today I am sober.

Those people who perhaps think AA stands for Automobile

Association are not so far off the mark. Alcoholics Anonymous answer distress calls after the body and mind have suffered a breakdown and help tow you back to health and sanity.

I am still in the early stages of my recovery but have discovered enough about Alcoholics Anonymous to urge anybody with a drink problem to get in touch with them as quickly as possible. They need have no fears of being made to look weak, embarrassed, humble or shameful. It takes strength of character and enormous will power to beat the illness and the AA is an organisation of ordinary everyday people who can feed fellow alcoholics with the confidence needed to stand up and fight against their problem. Above all, anybody contacting the AA will get *understanding*. Only another alocholic can understand the fears, anxieties and doubts of an alcoholic.

Let me tell you a little about Alcoholics Anonymous. I promise to try not to bore you. All I hope is that what you read here may help you or perhaps somebody you know who has the problem to get a grasp of what AA is about. If I can help just one other alcoholic back from hell by introducing him or her to Alcoholics Anonymous then all the misery and torment I have been through these last five years will not have been totally in vain.

Before starting this book, I looked up the latest official Government health figures on alcoholism. It was estimated that at least 500,000 people in Britain alone are addicted to alcohol. I hope my experiences convince at least some of them that the AA are an organisation that can help towards recovery and rehabilitation.

Alcoholics Anonymous started more or less by accident in America in 1935. Bill W., a stockbroker with a drink problem, found his desire to hit the bottle lessened when he was trying to talk other drunks out of the habit which he fully realised was harmful to the body and soul. While on a visit to Akron in Ohio he met up with Bob S., a doctor who was also suffering from the destructive forces of alcoholism. By helping each other in their weaker moments, they gradually beat the habit and decided to look for other alcoholics to help with words of encouragement.

There are now more than one-million AA members in the United States and more than 28,000 AA Fellowship groups throughout the world. New members are accepted without question. There is no entrance examination, no entrance fee or initiation ceremony and no surnames are ever used so all members retain their anonymity. Some groups use the sponsorship system, with 'established' members introducing newcomers and acting as guides and mentors during the early days of rehabilitation. But then there are groups like the one to which I belong in Brentwood where new members are encouraged to stand on their own two feet right from the first meeting but with fellow-members always prepared to be called on for help in moments of weakness and crisis.

We have two types of meetings. One is 'closed' for members only, with a volunteer chairman introducing a subject for discussion about different problems of alcoholism during which we talk about our experiences and exchange points of view. Then there are 'open' meetings for members and non-alcoholic guests at which there are generally two or three main speakers and 'outsiders' can see how we work together to cure our problem.

Once the alcoholic accepts that the AA is there to help but not interfere, he or she is always impressed by hearing people discussing the problems of drink in a language they understand as their own. They find that their fellow members have been through similar, even identical, experiences to their own which they thought nobody else on earth could have suffered. They are not criticised or patronised but are *understood*.

I say this in all sincerity – I have never ever before experienced the feeling of love, togetherness and companionship that I have found in the AA. There is no bar to any race, creed or colour. Christians, Jews, white, black, yellow. We all meet together in fellowship and are bound by one common bond. We are all alcoholics, all of us in various stages of rehabilitation and helping each other along the long road back to recovery. We are in no way freaks but have a human failing of which we are aware and which we aim to overcome together.

Each member of the AA tackles the following Programme of Recovery which is called The Twelve Steps:

We –
1. Admitted we were powerless over alcohol – that our lives had become unmanageable.
2. Came to believe that a Power greater than ourselves could restore us to sanity.
3. Made a decision to turn our will and our lives over to the care of God as we understood Him.
4. Made a searching and fearless moral inventory of ourselves.
5. Admitted to God, to ourselves, and to another human being the exact nature of our wrongs.
6. Were entirely ready to have God remove all these defects of character.
7. Humbly asked Him to remove our shortcomings.
8. Made a list of all persons we had harmed and became willing to make amends to them all.
9. Made direct amends to such people wherever possible, except when to do so would injure them or others.
10. Continued to take a personal inventory and, when we were wrong, promptly admitted it.
11. Sought through power of prayer and meditation to improve our conscious contact with God as we understood Him, praying only for knowledge of His will for us and the power to carry that out.
12. Having had a spiritual experience as a result of these steps, tried to carry this message to alcoholics and to practise these principles in all our affairs.

(From Alcoholics Anonymous, Copyright © Alcoholic Anonymous World Services Inc.)

I have never been one to beat the drum for religion. I respect, even envy those who find strength and faith through the Church but I have deep-set doubts about the workings and philosophy of the Church in today's modern world. But that is not to say that I am not a religious person. I do believe that somevhere there is a Power greater than ourselves. The human being is such a weak animal in most cases that I am sure that there has just got to be somebody or something with a superior mind and intelligence. I follow my religion not in a church but carry it around with me in my heart and my head.

Since joining the AA, I have become much more aware of my spiritual well being and I am stronger willed and more purposeful because of it. At least for today.

I was raised as a Roman Catholic and used to occasionally go to church during England tours with my old mate Nobby Stiles, who may have been something of a demon on the pitch but off it was a very religious, responsible and serious young man. But apart from weddings, Christenings and funerals, I have rarely been a regular churchgoer since my schooldays.

It may not please those Irish goalkeepers against whom I scored ten of my forty-four international goals to learn that I come from Irish stock. I looked into my family background in the mistaken belief that my drinking problem could be hereditary. My mother and father rarely drink and I have an elder brother and sister, both with teaching degrees, who are perfectly sober people. In fact 'Sis' has recently become a headmistress which proves she has got a responsible head on her shoulders. And my Dad had always to keep a clear mind for his job as a train driver on the London Underground.

I began to put the hereditary theory together when I discovered that my maternal grandfather used to give the bottle a good hammering. He was a very heavy drinker, putting away pints like nobody's business but stopped short of becoming an alcoholic. In the language of those days he was 'a bit of a lad'. Could I have caught the drinking bug from him? Well this notion has been kicked into touch by a procession of qualified psychiatrists who are convinced that alcoholism is not inherited. They point out that we inherit genes but not characters. The craving for alcohol cannot be transmitted in the egg or sperm. So I've only got myself to blame for my condition. And only I can cure it, with the help of my friends at the AA.

Now that I am living alone and no longer spending hours at

a time in pubs, I have become a 'screenaholic'. At the end of each day I while away my evenings in my little bachelor flat watching television. It helps me cut off and get through each day. My difficult times come when I am watching commercial TV.

Only an alcoholic seeking to become cured could tell you just how much of our screen time is taken up by adverts for booze ...

There's that bloke in the desert again dying for a beer. Now he's got a pint of iced lager in his hands and is sipping it like a big pouf. I would get through that in two seconds flat. I could really go a pint of that lager, Jimbo. But not today, eh ...

Those adverts become evil seducers for alcoholics. What I don't like about them is that too often they give the impression that drink can make you a better person, irresistible to the opposite sex and more successful in life. I am living proof that in every instance the opposite is in fact the case. Somebody should make them tell the truth about drink and its possible side effects. Cigarettes carry a Government health warning. Why not drink?

These days, away from the television set and my new circle of friends in the AA, I spend my time in the football season as a proud member of the Barnet team in the Southern League. I don't say proud to be patronising but because I really mean it. Barnet are a great little club and I am more than thankful to them for continuing to have faith in me despite my problem. I am enjoying my football more than ever before in my life. It is a release valve from all the tensions and pressures, the opposite of when I used to be a First Division footballer. In those days it was the cause of many of my problems and I turned to drink as a crutch. Now I am leaning heavily on football to help me through my crisis.

At the peak of my playing career, people used to think I took the game almost casually in my stride without worries or concern. In actual fact I lived on my nerves as a player and deep inside wasn't the confident, assured bloke that I appeared to be on the pitch.

Until you have competed at the highest level of the game you cannot possibly appreciate and understand the pressures and stress that the modern professional is under. You often read about showbiz and theatrical people turning to the bottle as escapism from the strains of their profession. Well I believe footballers in the top sphere are under even more strain.

Richard Burton, for instance, can learn his lines that somebody else has written for him and walk on stage and convey the words to the audience perhaps better than anybody else in the world. He will rightfully get applause and acclaim at the end of his performance. But just remember that the audience were with him right from the first curtain and his supporting cast were working with him, speaking their lines at exactly the moment that they had been rehearsing for weeks.

Footballers rehearse their movements for weeks but when they go on *their* stage the audience is often against them and there are eleven other blokes doing their best to stop them from playing. It's difficult to give a star performance if one of your co-stars has just been kicked into touch by a giant defender in size ten boots. I wonder how the wonderfully talented Richard Burton would get on if somebody was trying to kick him in the shins every time he went to deliver a line?

Something else they don't have in the theatre making life harder is a whistle-happy referee or a coach screaming from the touchline bench. 'Break his f------ leg ...' Yes, I've heard that shouted from touchline benches before now by opposition coaches trying to put the fear of hell into players.

I didn't used to be frightened on the football pitch. But I was always relieved to get off in one piece, particularly during those mid and late 1960s when the likes of Leeds United were kicking anything that moved.

Now I'm happily playing a midfield role for Barnet, spraying passes around Rivelino-style. I leave the goal scoring to others. I did my fair share of that in the First Division.

There has been a marvellous private and public reaction to

I must have posed in more than a hundred team photographs since I first started kicking a football but this one has special significance because it's my very *first* team picture. I'm the first boy on the left in the back row, the nipper of the South Wood Lane School Under-10s team. This photo was taken after we had won the Dagenham schools league title. We went for the 'double' but were beaten in the cup final. The pressure had started!

Two players from this 1957 Middlesex County youth team were posing for a battery of photographers with the England World Cup squad in 1966. That's me with the ball at my feet in the middle of the front row. Can you spot the other player who later established himself in the England team? I'll give you a clue – he wore the no. 2 shirt in the 1966 World Cup Final. It's George Cohen, of course, sitting two along to my right in the front row.

Every picture tells a story and this one taken at Heathrow Airport in 1961 could have provided a few thousand words for Italian reporters. Desmond Hackett and I have just realised that the plane taking me to Milan for my first match with the Italian club has departed without us. We had already polished off a bottle of champers with a lobster lunch. Dear old Des, the legendary 'Man in the Brown Bowler' of the *Daily Express*, had the answer to our dilemma. He ordered another bottle of champagne! Meantime all hell had let loose in Milan where they thought I had changed my mind about joining them. There was a club reception committee waiting for me along with more than fifty reporters, photographers and TV cameramen. I turned up three hours later than scheduled and at a different airport. It was just as well there were not too many witnesses to my arrival. I had ploughed into more champers on the plane to ease my paranoic fear of flying. By the time we touched down, I was really flying high. Cheers Des!

This is how I looked in my first season in League football with Chelsea – 1957–8. Note the baggy shorts, bulky shinpads and heavy, ankle-high boots. The streamlined look had not yet reached English soccer.

It wasn't all misery in Milan. I enjoyed this pre-match reunion with my England team-mate Gerry Hitchens. He was playing for our deadly rivals Inter-Milan. Our coach Rocco almost had apoplexy when he saw me shaking hands with Gerry. He would rather have seen me shaking my fist at him. I am pleased for Gerry that he settled into Italian football much better than I ever did and played with distinction for Torino and Cagliari before returning to England as a non-League footballer.

The lovely little bundle I'm holding is the reason I was late joining Milan. I refused to move to Italy until Mitzi had arrived. This photograph was taken after we had moved into our flat in Milan. Irene, then Mrs Greaves, has got lovely Lyn on her lap. I'm in charge of Mitzi. Both have grown into beautiful young ladies who make me feel very old every time I see them – which, I am happy to say, is often.

This *Daily Express* picture by Norman Quicke captures a typical AC Milan 'walkabout' training session. That's coach Nero Rocco leading the way. We used to walk for miles with the objective of relaxing our minds and our muscles. All it did was bore us out of our minds. That's Jose Altafini, a genius of a Brazilian player, stifling a yawn. I'm nibbling my nails and no doubt day dreaming about a frothy pint of English beer. Seeing this photograph of Rocco reminds me of a lovely Des Hackett story. He described Rocco in the *Express* as looking like a pot-bellied heavyweight boxer. This was translated to Rocco who went angrily in search of Des. 'Which one Desmond 'ackett?' he demanded in broken English as he approached a posse of English journalists. Des pointed him in the direction of an open-mouthed colleague and then did a Houdini-style disappearing act.

A lot of people will disagree but I rate this the best of all the post-war England teams. Reading left to right in the back row are Jimmy Armfield, Bobby Robson, Peter Swan, Ron Springett, Ron Flowers, Mick McNeil and reserve Brian Miller. Then in the front row, certainly the best international attack I ever played in, Bryan Douglas, little me, Bobby Smith, Johnny Haynes and Bobby Charlton. On the flanks are team manager Walter Winterbottom, who seems to be doing some finger stretching exercises, and loyal trainer Harold Shepherdson. If you could have put this 1961 forward line together with the 1966 England World Cup defence, you would have had an unbeatable combination.

Here comes one of the most satisfying goals of my career. I am just taking
the ball around Yugoslav goalkeeper Soskic to give England a 2–1 win
against the Rest of the World in the FA Centenary match at Wembley in
1963. Soskic had come on as a second-half substitute for legendary
Russian goalkeeper Lev Yashin who had made three blinding saves against
me in the first-half. I got the ball past Yashin once after beating four
players in a 20-yard run but Scottish referee Bobby Davidson blew up for
a free-kick because I'd been fouled just outside the penalty area. I was
choked that he had not played the advantage rule and later described it
as the best goal I never got!

My first altercation with Alf Ramsey. He's giving me a rollicking here for
sky-larking during an England training session. This was taken the day
before his first match as England manager against France in Paris. I was
never able to give total concentration to training and Alf told me ever so
politely that he had a job to do and would appreciate my full co-
operation. The next evening we got hammered 5–2 by France in a
pantomime of a match. It was the night poor Ron Springett kept losing
the ball in the glare of the floodlights. It was three years before we got our
revenge, beating France 2–0 at Wembley in 1966 in my last World Cup
match.

I suppose this could be described as being taken at the peak of my career during my first season with Spurs. This was before a mixture of age and alcohol started to knock the edge off my speed and reflexes. The summertime of my life.

They always used to say I thought my head was only for putting my hat on but here's picture proof that I could nod them in. Tommy Lawton would have been proud of this one as I go up at the far post to head in a Cliffie Jones cross against Sheffield United. The goal had special significance because it was my thirty-seventh First Division goal of the 1962–3 season which is still a club record at Tottenham.

I must have posed in more than a hundred team photographs since I first started kicking a football but this one has special significance because it's my very *first* team picture. I'm the first boy on the left in the back row, the nipper of the South Wood Lane School Under-10s team. This photo was taken after we had won the Dagenham schools league title. We went for the 'double' but were beaten in the cup final. The pressure had started!

Two players from this 1957 Middlesex County youth team were posing for a battery of photographers with the England World Cup squad in 1966. That's me with the ball at my feet in the middle of the front row. Can you spot the other player who later established himself in the England team? I'll give you a clue – he wore the no. 2 shirt in the 1966 World Cup Final. It's George Cohen, of course, sitting two along to my right in the front row.

Every picture tells a story and this one taken at Heathrow Airport in 1961 could have provided a few thousand words for Italian reporters. Desmond Hackett and I have just realised that the plane taking me to Milan for my first match with the Italian club has departed without us. We had already polished off a bottle of champers with a lobster lunch. Dear old Des, the legendary 'Man in the Brown Bowler' of the *Daily Express*, had the answer to our dilemma. He ordered another bottle of champagne! Meantime all hell had let loose in Milan where they thought I had changed my mind about joining them. There was a club reception committee waiting for me along with more than fifty reporters, photographers and TV cameramen. I turned up three hours later than scheduled and at a different airport. It was just as well there were not too many witnesses to my arrival. I had ploughed into more champers on the plane to ease my paranoic fear of flying. By the time we touched down, I was really flying high. Cheers Des!

This is how I looked in my first season in League football with Chelsea – 1957–8. Note the baggy shorts, bulky shinpads and heavy ankle-high boots. The streamlined look had not yet reached English soccer.

It wasn't all misery in Milan. I enjoyed this pre-match reunion with my England team-mate Gerry Hitchens. He was playing for our deadly rivals Inter-Milan. Our coach Rocco almost had apoplexy when he saw me shaking hands with Gerry. He would rather have seen me shaking my fist at him. I am pleased for Gerry that he settled into Italian football much better than I ever did and played with distinction for Torino and Cagliari before returning to England as a non-League footballer.

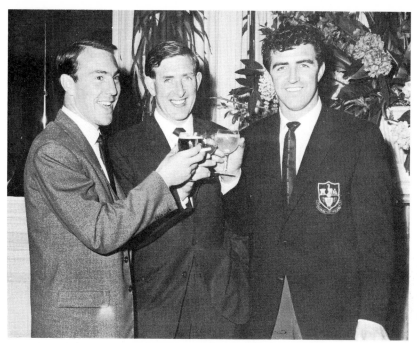

A favourite pose of mine before Alcoholics Anonymous helped pull me straight. The glass of beer and cigarette were constantly at hand in my off-pitch moments. Teetotaller Danny Blanchflower in the middle is content with an orange juice. Bobby Smith is into a glass of his favourite gin and tonic. This picture was taken after each of us had scored in Tottenham's 3–1 FA Cup Final victory against Burnley at Wembley in 1962.

Here's a picture that has pride of place in my photo album. That footballing genius Sir Stanley Matthews invited me to play for his All Star team against an international select side. It was the occasion of his testimonial at Stoke in 1965. He was then fifty and still able to run the legs off players half his age. Sir Stanley, a fitness fanatic, non-smoker and teetotaller, will shake his head in a mixture of disbelief and dismay when he hears of my drinking exploits. I would rather youngsters copied his approach to the game than mine

This is me being flippant about my businessman image. Eat your heart out Patrick Macnee of the Avengers! The picture was taken after I had become a member of Lloyds, a sign of the respect and money I had earned in the business world.

I enjoyed the image of the pipe-puffing business executive and in my later playing years took it more seriously than my football. This photograph was taken in my office in 1966. Yes, I'm a left-hander and favoured my left foot when shooting for goal.

Ride him cowboy! This is my lovely old dog Bruno, a St Bernard we used to have. There is no truth in the rumour that we kept him so that I could raid the brandy bottle around his neck. On my head is one of the fifty-seven England caps I won. Lester Piggott will like the style but I'm not so sure about the Football Association!

They say comedians always want to play Hamlet. Likewise, strikers always fancy themselves as goalkeepers. I was never in the Gordon Banks class but saved a few in my time as an emergency keeper. This picture was taken after one of my failures. Photographer Norman Quicke has just put a penalty past me in a Sunday afternoon match.

Following in father's footsteps, one. This is Andrew, aged two, getting an early lesson in ball control from a proud dad who thinks he knows a thing or two about it. The showcase is a museum of all the things I won in football. Andrew is now twelve and developing nicely as a player in schools football.

Following in father's footsteps, two. This is Andrew nine years later getting dad's tactical advice before a schoolboys' match. I was into a drinking decline when this picture was taken but in my sober moments was always on the touchline to give my boys, Danny and Andrew, a father's encouragement. Danny is now fifteen and a junior player on Tottenham's books. I have high hopes for him and just pray he has learned from his dad's mistakes.

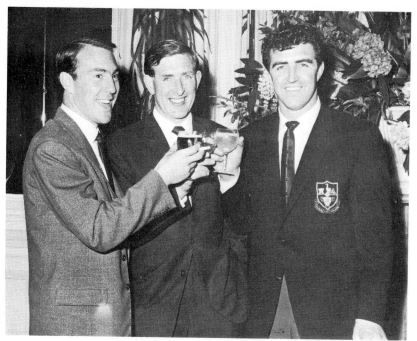

A favourite pose of mine before Alcoholics Anonymous helped pull me straight. The glass of beer and cigarette were constantly at hand in my off-pitch moments. Teetotaller Danny Blanchflower in the middle is content with an orange juice. Bobby Smith is into a glass of his favourite gin and tonic. This picture was taken after each of us had scored in Tottenham's 3–1 FA Cup Final victory against Burnley at Wembley in 1962.

Here's a picture that has pride of place in my photo album. That footballing genius Sir Stanley Matthews invited me to play for his All Star team against an international select side. It was the occasion of his testimonial at Stoke in 1965. He was then fifty and still able to run the legs off players half his age. Sir Stanley, a fitness fanatic, non-smoker and teetotaller, will shake his head in a mixture of disbelief and dismay when he hears of my drinking exploits. I would rather youngsters copied his approach to the game than mine

This is me being flippant about my businessman image. Eat your heart out Patrick Macnee of the Avengers! The picture was taken after I had become a member of Lloyds, a sign of the respect and money I had earned in the business world.

I enjoyed the image of the pipe-puffing business executive and in my later playing years took it more seriously than my football. This photograph was taken in my office in 1966. Yes, I'm a left-hander and favoured my left foot when shooting for goal.

Ride him cowboy! This is my lovely old dog Bruno, a St Bernard we used to have. There is no truth in the rumour that we kept him so that I could raid the brandy bottle around his neck. On my head is one of the fifty-seven England caps I won. Lester Piggott will like the style but I'm not so sure about the Football Association!

They say comedians always want to play Hamlet. Likewise, strikers always fancy themselves as goalkeepers. I was never in the Gordon Banks class but saved a few in my time as an emergency keeper. This picture was taken after one of my failures. Photographer Norman Quicke has just put a penalty past me in a Sunday afternoon match.

Following in father's footsteps, one. This is Andrew, aged two, getting an early lesson in ball control from a proud dad who thinks he knows a thing or two about it. The showcase is a museum of all the things I won in football. Andrew is now twelve and developing nicely as a player in schools football.

Following in father's footsteps, two. This is Andrew nine years later getting dad's tactical advice before a schoolboys' match. I was into a drinking decline when this picture was taken but in my sober moments was always on the touchline to give my boys, Danny and Andrew, a father's encouragement. Danny is now fifteen and a junior player on Tottenham's books. I have high hopes for him and just pray he has learned from his dad's mistakes.

my confession of being an alcoholic. I've had hundreds of letters of support, sympathy and understanding from close friends and also from strangers who I have never met but identify with me through football.

I expected a lot of banter from the terraces when the facts of my problem were made public and sure enough the comedians are out in force but are rarely nasty with their shouts. 'Fancy a beer, Jim?' ... 'Mind you don't hit the bar, Greavsie' ... 'Pissed again, Jim!' (when I miss a sitter). These seem to be the favourites but they are aimed at me in good humoured fashion.

During a match at Yeovil, one fan wasn't too pleased with me after I had won the ball in a tackle (whoever thought they would hear Jimmy Greaves talking about winning a tackle!). The supporter yelled: 'You drunken bum, Greaves ...'

I turned to one of the Yeovil players and said 'He's right, y'know. But I don't know what that makes you lot because we're winning ...!'

There are quite a few of my old acquaintances who are convinced I will soon be back on the bottle. They don't harbour these thoughts in a malicious way but have been so accustomed to seeing me under the influence of drink during the past five years that they are sure I am hooked on the habit for life.

They don't know it but their attitude is helping me in my battle. My pride is telling me I must try to prove them wrong.

I would dearly love to wipe the last five or six years out of my life and go back to the way we were. But that is a passing thought that I must kick into touch immediately. The past is the past and I cannot turn the clock back. I would just like to ask the forgiveness and understanding of any people I may have harmed, hurt or let down during my five lost years.

In the AA at times of crisis and weakening, we have a saying: 'If you cannot go without a drink for a day at a time, make it for an hour at a time ...'

I am determined not to go back to the degradation and

the demoralisation I experienced at the rock bottom of my life.

For the next hour I shall be sober. And for the rest of the day.

Just for today.

9

Read all about it

'On behalf of the British Press ...'
– Roy Peskett (ex-*Daily Mail*)

It wasn't all drinking, of course. I did manage to play some football between rounds. And I loved every minute of it. Well, at least most of the minutes.

I wish to place on record my thanks to the British Pressmen who reported my footballing fortunes around the world, most of them favourably, just a few inaccurately and one or two of them with imaginations that far outstripped the facts.

Thanks to them and the painstaking cutting-and-pasting work of my mum and dad and, most of all, Irene, I have thirty scrapbooks containing an All Our Yesterdays reminder of the moments that mattered in my career.

Come with me down the road to yesterday and see what memories the stories conjure up. It will be a last look over my shoulder before giving total concentration to my new way of life ...

Jimmy Greaves gave the greatest show I have ever seen from a young player in his League debut and I have seen the juvenile performances of soccer starlets Johnny Haynes and Duncan Edwards. Tottenham's Danny Blanchflower said after 17-year-old Greaves had snatched a late equaliser for Chelsea, 'The boy is a natural. He is the greatest youngster I have ever played against.'

That was how Desmond Hackett reported my League debut for Chelsea at White Hart Lane in the *Daily Express* on 25 August 1957. I remember before the game having a pair of shorts thrown to me that came down past my knees. They would have been big enough for Bobby Smith, even Cyril Smith! But I was too nervous about the game to make any protest and from then on refused to part with those 'lucky' shorts. Everybody thought I was copying Alex James who had become a legend at Arsenal with his baggy shorts but it had not been planned.

Here's how Jim Gaughan, of that great old London evening paper, *The Star*, reported my England Under-23 debut on 25 September 1957:

More than 56,000 people at Stamford Bridge were shown that Johnny Haynes and Jimmy Greaves are natural partners. There has been nothing quite like this from an England pair since the great days of Raich Carter and Wilf Mannion. Greaves, making his Under-23 international debut, scored twice and missed a penalty during an eventful first match in which England crushed Bulgaria 6–2 ...

Of all my partnerships in football, I rated this one with Johnny Haynes the best. It was as if we were made for each other. I recall Geoffrey Green, the Association Football correspondent of *The Times*, remarking once that, 'It was a partnership made in Heaven.' If I can deviate for just one moment and talk about dear old Geoffrey Green. What a character! He writes like a poet and can charm the birds down out of the trees with his lyrical speeches. Happiness to Geoffrey is a brimming glass and footballing company. He loves the game and has done it a great service over the years with his authoritative and wonderfully descriptive reporting in *The Times* and on BBC radio. Geoffrey is a Corinthian gentleman who used to play universities football. He somehow managed to be born in India but is English to the core.

I have spent many enjoyable hours in his company and one story that stands out in my memory is of when during an England tour match in Poland he and Laurie Pignon, then on the *Daily Sketch*, were arrested for causing some disturbance in a city centre. As I was told it, Geoffrey was making a public speech about the values of a free society and Laurie, who had been given a rough time as a prisoner of war in Poland, was seconding the argument. I think it fair to say that both were quite well lubricated. Two guards, in ankle-length fur-lined coats, appeared from out of nowhere and marched Geoffrey and Laurie away. A few hours later, with their worried Press colleagues wondering whether to call in the British ambassador, they reappeared wearing broad, drunken grins and, would you believe, a fur-lined ankle-length guardsman's coat each! Geoffrey continued to wear his coveted coat in the Press boxes of the world right up until his retirement a couple of years ago as the man from *The Times*. I don't think loveable Laurie Pignon would consider wearing his in the Wimbledon Press box in his role as lawn tennis correspondent for the *Daily Mail*.

Just one more Geoffrey Green story before I dip back into my scrapbooks. When a testimonial dinner was organised for Sir Alf Ramsey, Geoffrey followed the then Prime Minister Harold Wilson as speaker. Geoffrey brought the house down by suggesting that Sir Alf join him in a busking team and then proceeded to play 'Moon River' on a mouth organ. I don't know who was more surprised, Sir Alf or the Prime Minister. Over the rainbow, Geoff baby!

Peter Lorenzo, an old Essex acquaintance of mine, was working on the *Daily Herald* when he wrote this match report on 26 December 1957:

The phenomenal Jimmy Greaves gave Portsmouth a Christmas socking with four of Chelsea's seven goals at Stamford Bridge. It was a case of many happy returns for Greaves who had been rested by manager Ted Drake because 'he's too good to hurry'.

Those were the days when we used to play football on Christmas Day and I was back in the first-team after a six-week break. Manager Ted Drake had been worried that I was getting too much publicity and pressure and after I had gone a run of six games without scoring he told me to take a complete break from the game. It was supposed to have been a two-week rest but it stretched to more than a month because Chelsea hit a winning sequence without me. The four-goal comeback was the best Christmas present I could have given myself. Chelsea did not drop me again after that.

The late J. G. Orange, a distinguished Victorian-looking gentleman who used to wear a rose in his overcoat lapel, reported in the London *Evening News* of 30 August 1958:

> Chelsea bombarded League champions Wolves with six goals at Stamford Bridge this afternoon – and Jimmy Greaves scored five of them. He netted a good-looking sixth, only to be ruled offside.

I have been told that this was the day Billy Wright decided he would hang up his boots at the end of the season. We really gave Wolves the run around and the Wolves and England skipper had a nightmare match. I played in the last three matches of Billy's magnificent 105-cap international career and found him a lovely bloke who went out of his way to make me feel comfortable as a newcomer to the England squad. Wolves along with Manchester United had been the dominant side of the 1950s but we caught them on the downhill run that afternoon at Stamford Bridge.

Ian Wooldridge, a genius at the word game, was an up-and-coming reporter on the old *News Chronicle* when he saw me play for Chelsea against Nottingham Forest on 26 September 1958 BC – Before Clough:

> Two prods and a nod gave Jimmy Greaves a hat-trick against Nottingham Forest and put him out on his own as the League's top scorer with 16 goals. The season is only 10 games old and the mind boggles at thoughts of what his goals haul will be when the shooting and the shouting is over·...

Every player has his 'rabbit' team. Forest were mine. I was always for some reason able to turn it on against them. And it wasn't as if they were a bad side in those days. Among their prominent players of the time I can recall Bobby McKinlay, Jack Burkitt, Jeff Whitefoot, Stewart Imlach, Johnny Quigley, Billy Gray, Tommy Wilson and little Roy Dwight who has since become famous as Elton John's uncle. And dear old Eddie Baily had a spell with Forest after leaving Spurs. They won the FA Cup at the end of the season by beating Luton Town in the Final at Wembley. For a bloke whose memory is supposed to have 'gone' I'm doing well. It just shows the value of keeping newspaper cuttings.

And here's one from the *Daily Mirror* dated 2 April 1959, reporter George Harley:

Jimmy Greaves at last managed to slip past Arsenal skipper Dave Bowen to calmly score an equaliser. So, at 19, Greaves has equalled the Chelsea record of 30 League goals in a season. And that was a target beyond the likes even of Tommy Lawton.

I finished that season with thirty-two goals but as fast as we banged them in at one end, our defence would open the doors at the back and let the opposition in. We scored seventy-seven goals but conceded ninety-eight. They were crazy days at Chelsea.

The England selectors picked me for the summer tour, which left a lot to be desired both on and off the pitch. It was poorly organised and our travel schedule would have worn out even Captain Cook. This was how David Jack, of the *Empire News*, reported my debut (have you noticed how many of the newspapers I'm quoting from have gone out of business? Fleet Street seems a dodgy old place to me):

Jimmy Greaves, making his international debut for England against Peru in Lima, scored the first of what will surely be many goals for his country. His performance was a rare bright spot in a humiliating 4–1 defeat that once again emphasised that drastic changes must be made at the top. Make no mistake, this is crisis time for England. The game we gave to the world is no longer played with the required skill by English footballers...

Nothing changes! It seems ridiculous to make excuses at

this distance but we were honestly worn out by the travelling we had to do. We played Brazil, Peru, Mexico and the United States during a span of fifteen days. We were beaten 2–0 by world champions Brazil, 4–1 by a Peruvian side that was packed with highly-skilled players and then 2–1 by Mexico in the high altitude of Mexico City. We took all our frustration out on the United States and hammered them 8–1, with Bobby Charlton helping himself to a hat-trick. I could and should have had about five goals and finished up with none! Three of the players in our eighteen-man squad – Roy Gratrix, Graham Shaw and Ron Baynham – travelled halfway round the world without getting a kick at a ball and Wilf McGuinness got on for only forty-five minutes. It was my first close-up look at international football from the inside. I was not impressed.

Back to the bread-and-butter business of League football with Chelsea and this was how James Connolly reported one of our more spectacular victories in his *Sunday Express* round-up column of 19 December 1959:

Jimmy Greaves, brilliant young Chelsea inside-left, toppled Preston off the top of the table with all five goals in a stunning success at Deepdale. Chelsea won a thrilling, see-sawing match 5–4, with all the glory belonging to Greaves who at times seemed to be playing them on his own.

It's interesting to see Jim Connolly referring to me as an inside-left. People have often asked me whether I considered myself an inside-left or inside-right. I just preferred to be known as an inside-forward. The number of the shirt never really mattered to me. I've always been a no. 8 or no. 10 man but have never consciously tried to favour the left or right side of the field. My aim was always to take the shortest possible route to goal. I have usually favoured my left foot for shooting but like to think I can be equally accurate with my right if the circumstances demand it.

I obviously impressed *Daily Express* reporter Bob Pennington – now a leading columnist in Canada – with my performance for England Under-23s on 1 March 1960:

Magnificent ... uncanny ... superb ... shattering. That was Jimmy Greaves at Ibrox last night with a hat-trick for Young England that was one of the finest seen in this hallowed home of Glasgow Rangers ...

I couldn't have put it better myself! Among my team-mates that evening were George Cohen, Maurice Setters, Peter Swan, Tony Kay, George Eastham and Bobby Charlton. Scotland included Adam Blacklaw, Jimmy Gabriel, Ian St John and Denis Law. Despite what the critics were saying, our game wasn't in such bad shape. These players were as good as any Under-23s in the world.

The late Bill Holden, a respected reporter with the *Daily Mirror*, saw me among the goals again on 6 September 1960:

Jimmy Greaves, the Chelsea goal-charmer with genius in his boots, paraded all his match-winning magnificence against Blackburn last night as he scored his second hat-trick of the season.

But it was still like a circus at Chelsea. That season we scored seventy-six goals and conceded ninety-one. The next season we really surpassed ourselves with a haul of ninety-eight goals. Trouble was that our defence let in a hundred! Can you wonder that I reckoned I might be doing myself a favour to move on to a new club?

Frank McGhee, now the pungent columnist on the *Daily Mirror*, was in Luxembourg to report on our World Cup qualifying match on 19 October 1960:

Jimmy Greaves, as dramatic as sudden death, responded magnificently to the demands of captain-general Johnny Haynes. Greaves and Bobby Charlton, a blond bomb in boots, scored three goals each in this ruthless 9–0 triumph over Luxembourg.

It was about this time that I was beginning to think that a move would help my career, as Clive Toye – now a soccer executive in the United States – reported in the *Daily Express* of 4 November 1960:

Jimmy Greaves, of Chelsea and England, the greatest goal-scoring inside-forward of modern times, wants a transfer. He says: 'I want to try my luck with another club. Chelsea have great potential but, for some reason, it is not being properly fulfilled.'

This started a long-running series of will-they-won't-they-sell-him stories that kept my name prominent on the back pages of all the national newspapers. But I was still finding the net with a fair ratio of shots in what was my best-ever season for goal scoring. This is how the late Ralph Hadley reported one of my milestones in *The People* on 4 December 1960:

Jimmy Greaves scored five goals in this 7–1 thrashing of West Brom ... the 12th time that he has scored three or more in a match. He has become the youngest player at 20 to total 100 League goals and has scored 11 times in 11 appearances for England. How on earth can Chelsea even think of selling him?

I'm enjoying these scrapbook memories. Did I really score all those goals? To be honest, goal scoring came so naturally to me that I didn't realise I was doing anything particularly astonishing. But now that I look back in my old age ('You'll be forty soon, Jimbo!') and judging it by today's goal standard I suppose I must have been a bit special.

Tom Holley was *The People* reporter at Stamford Bridge when Chelsea played Newcastle United. It was just before this First Division match that a Newcastle official told me the club would pay me a signing-on bonus of £1000 and give me a £50-a-week car salesman's job if I agreed to join them:

A wonder show of goal snatching by Jimmy Greaves just about put paid to Newcastle's hopes of staving off relegation. He crashed into top gear with four brilliant goals as Chelsea helped themselves to six in twenty-eight fantastic minutes.

Clive Toye was the first newspaperman to link my name with AC Milan in the *Daily Express*. Bernard Joy, the last amateur to play in a full international for England and a respected football writer with the *Evening Standard*, followed up with the full facts:

Jimmy Greaves has signed for the crack Italian club AC Milan. He has signed an option drawn up by Chelsea and Milan, so that if the Italians lift the ban on imported players at the end of this month he will be a Milan player next season.

Four days later, Frank Butler – sports editor and columnist of the *News of the World* – was among the lucky people at Wembley who witnessed one of the greatest performances of all time by an England team. He reported on 11 August 1961:

There are some who will say Jimmy Greaves is worth £200,000 after the way he strolled through this 9–3 humiliation of Scotland at Wembley. He scored three goals and played a major role in three more.

The real star of that pulsating performance against a Scottish side including Dave Mackay, Denis Law and Ian St John was our skipper Johnny Haynes, who paralysed the Scots with his pin-pointed passes. He got two goals himself, with Bobby Smith (2), Bobby Robson and Bryan Douglas also getting in on the scoring act. An abiding memory is of Dave Mackay charging murderously at any Englishman in possession in the closing stages of the match. He carries the scar of that demoralising defeat to this day. England came close to perfection that afternoon. The pity was that we failed to reach double figures. That would have made a magic entry in the record books. The win was a vindication of a team policy that team manager Walter Winterbottom had adopted at the start of the season. He was determined to mould a settled side and pledged to keep the team unchanged provided, of course, everybody was playing reasonably well. He kept to his word and we won all five matches that season, scoring thirty-two goals and conceding only eight. At the end of the slaughter of the Scots, we carried Johnny Haynes around the pitch on our shoulders as if he was the FA Cup.

A couple of weeks later, on 28 April 1961, I was being carried around the Stamford Bridge pitch by Chelsea fans after I had played my last game for the club. James Connolly reported in his *Sunday Express* round-up column:

Jimmy Greaves was carried off in triumph after saying a four-goal farewell to the Chelsea fans. Greaves, captain for the day, clinched a dramatic 4–3 victory over Nottingham Forest with a last-minute penalty.

A couple of days later Chelsea and I had stopped waving fond farewells and were shaking our fists at each other instead, as Gerald Williams – now a leading figure in lawn tennis circles – reported in the *Daily Mail* of 1 May 1961:

Jimmy Greaves has lost his place in the England team for the next two matches because he refused to obey Chelsea's orders to join them on a close-season tour of Israel. He has been suspended for 14 days by the club.

It was a ridiculous over-reaction from Chelsea. Some months later chairman Joe Mears told me that the club could not be seen to being dictated to by a player and also that they had been invited to Israel on the understanding that I would be playing. I was advised I could have sued Chelsea for restraint of trade but I have never been the vindictive type and anyway, what was fourteen days to a twenty-year-old with his entire career before him?

I have two full scrapbooks on my Italian adventure and have picked out just a few of the stories to give an idea of the chaos and confusion it all caused ...

Jimmy Greaves flew into Italy at seven o'clock this morning to a passionate, hysterical welcome from his new club AC Milan. 'I had a wonderful farewell at Chelsea,' breathed Jimmy. 'But this welcome is even more fantastic. And I haven't even done anything yet.'

– Clive Toye, *Daily Express*, 2 May 1961

Mr J. H. Mears, Chelsea's chairman, yesterday broke his silence on the Greaves transfer negotiations to tell me of an astonishing offer should the deal with Milan fall through. Chelsea would pay Greaves a wage 'topping that of any other player in the League', if Milan did not exercise the option they have been given.

– J. L. Manning, *Daily Mail*, 12 May 1961

Eighty thousand jubilant Italians were silenced here in Rome's huge Olympic Stadium as two late goals by Gerry Hitchens and

Jimmy Greaves rescued England from their first international defeat for a year.

– John Camkin, *Daily Mail*, 24 May 1961

Jimmy Greaves said here in Vienna tonight that he is staying with Chelsea, turning down £10,000 from Milan and remaining with England's World Cup team. 'Steps are being taken to ensure that everything will be okay,' he revealed.

– Frank McGhee, *Daily Mirror*, 25 May 1961

Jimmy Greaves IS going to Milan. He today signed a personal contract with the Italian club here in Alassio. He is guaranteed earnings of at least £40,000 in the next three years. A five-figure part of that is to be paid immediately in a lump sum.

– Tony Stratton Smith, *Daily Sketch*, 2 June 1961

Fifty-thousand Milan fans filled out the giant San Siro Stadium here tonight delighted with the debut of Jimmy Greaves. And, true to custom, it had to be a scoring debut for the 21-year-old Cockney kid, who maintained his amazing record in this 2–2 draw with Botafogo of scoring in all his most important games.

– Peter Lorenzo, *Daily Herald*, 7 June 1961

Chelsea last night offered to pay £90,000 to get back Jimmy Greaves, the England inside-forward they sold for £80,000 only last April. This is the latest sensational development in the tangled story of the Cockney boy who sought a fortune in Italy – and found only bitter disillusion.

– Roy Peskett, *Daily Mail*, 18 October 1961

Jimmy Greaves drove away from Milan in his Jaguar car today to return home to England ready to start his new career as a £99,999 Tottenham player. 'I am not sorry to see the back of him,' said Milan coach Nero Rocco. 'He is a fine player but did not have his heart here.'

– Ronnie Waters, *Daily Sketch*, 24 November 1961

What that final *Daily Sketch* story failed to mention is that when I drove away from Milan for the last time the city was blanketed by the thickest fog I have ever experienced. Only people desperate to get somewhere were silly enough to drive in it – and I was desperate to get away from Italy. I left Milan at about five miles per hour.

It was Saturday 16 December 1961 when I made my debut for Tottenham at White Hart Lane. This is how my old Cockney mate, the late Victor Railton, reported it in the *Evening News*:

Jimmy Greaves made a sensational start to his career with Spurs this afternoon with a hat-trick against Blackpool at a packed White Hart Lane. So he kept up his habit of always scoring on big occasions and one of his goals was of the classic variety only he can produce. It came from an overhead scissors kick after Terry Medwin had flicked on a long throw from Dave Mackay. The Spurs fans loved it and gave Greaves a great ovation ...

Alan Hoby, a passionate writer on the *Sunday Express*, was a Press box observer of most of my most important matches. This is how he reported an FA Cup tie against West Bromwich Albion on 17 February 1962:

Incredible Tottenham Hotspur yesterday reached the last eight in the FA Cup when they beat West Brom before 55,000 stunned and astonished spectators. We saw two jinking Greaves goals, both of them great and both of them so memorable that they will be relished and cherished like old brandy.

Alan once had me falling about with laughter when he told me how he was trying to telephone a match report back to England from a Press box in Madrid. He found he had got a crossed line with a Spanish gentleman and politely asked him to get off the line. The Spaniard, equally polite, suggested that Alan should put his receiver down. Driven by a deadline that waits for no man, Alan began to scream at the Spaniard to clear the line. The Spaniard started to scream back. They were now shouting and raging at each other in their respective languages when one of Alan's colleagues noticed with interest that there were two gentlemen in the Press box bellowing in anger down their receivers. He drew Alan's attention to the man sitting two rows away cursing into his telephone in Spanish. It then dawned on Alan that this was the man he was arguing with and threatening with all sorts of physical torture. Somehow, they had their telephones plugged into the same line. Alan, like a true English gentleman, replaced his receiver and looked for another telephone to use.

I find that journalists are stacked with amusing anecdotes like this one and have had hours of entertainment from them in countless bars, nightclubs and hotel rooms around the world. Perhaps football writers should concentrate on writing their own memoirs instead of ghosting those of other people. Anyway, back to the scrapbooks . . .

Derek Wallis, the *Daily Mirror*'s chief football reporter in Manchester, reported on my return to the England Under-23 team on 28 February 1962:

Jimmy Greaves, back in an England shirt for the first time in nine months, completely shattered the Scots last night in this Under-23 international at Aberdeen. He was devastating, scoring two goals and making a third.

Tony Pawson, who had been an outstanding amateur player with that great Pegasus side of the 1950s, saw Tottenham reach the FA Cup Final for the second successive year on 30 March 1962, and reported in *The Observer*:

Spurs went marching serenely on to the FA Cup Final at Wembley, untroubled by Manchester United or the strains of the European Cup. Greaves took his vital goal with a sleepwalker's casual certainty, waiting for Gaskell to dive, then sliding the ball gently under him.

During my career I reckon I must have had more than a hundred goals disallowed for that most frustrating of all laws, offside. The one that hurt most of all was what I considered to be a perfectly good goal against Benfica in the European Cup semi-final first leg in Lisbon. This was how Roy Peskett reported it in the *Daily Mail* of 5 April 1962:

Jimmy Greaves, whose 'goal' in the 23rd minute was disallowed for offside, protested after Benfica had beaten Tottenham 4–3 on aggregate in the European Cup semi-final: 'I thought it was a good one. I ran between two Benfica players before shooting ...'

There is a legendary Fleet Street story about Roy Peskett, a cheerful and comical man who always seemed so fond of a flutter on the horses that I am sure he would have been happier as a racing correspondent. Journalists are often invited to pre-match receptions when on foreign tours and they usually elect one of their party to act as spokesman to officially thank their hosts for the invitation. These receptions can be hard-drinking affairs, particularly behind the Iron Curtain where they believe in drinking a toast to anything that moves. On this particular occasion, Roy had been elected spokesman at an East German reception that dragged on and on and on. Finally, after a dozen or more toasts, it was Roy's turn to make his short speech. It was probably the briefest speech of all time. Roy pulled himself unsteadily to his feet, uttered the immortal words 'On behalf of the British Press ...' and then collapsed back into his chair.

Roy Peskett ... Desmond Hackett ... Geoffrey Green ... Victor Railton ... J. L. Manning ... all of them rich with talent and great character and wit. The Press boxes will never be the same without them.

Those early European Cup matches with Tottenham were among the most memorable I have ever played in. This was how David Miller reported our eventual exit to Benfica in the *Daily Telegraph* of 5 April 1962:

At the end of a titantic drama, which left the nerves trembling, the throat dry, mighty Tottenham Hotspur, the pride of England, bowed out of the European Cup to the magnificent champions Benfica at White Hart Lane. Never, never was there such a match in England, or for that matter anywhere, said some who have followed this great international game round the globe ...'

We finished third in the League that season behind Alf Ramsey's shock Ipswich side and polished Burnley but found consolation in the FA Cup Final as Sam Leitch – now head of sport at Thames TV – reported in the *Sunday Pictorial* of 5 May 1962:

It was the opportunism of Jimmy Greaves after just 180 seconds that put Spurs in complete command of the FA Cup Final against Burnley. How he got that goal still mystifies me. A hefty clearance from goalkeeper Bill Brown was nodded down perfectly by Bobby Smith to the galloping feet of Greaves. He charged on to goal but lost control through the momentum of his own pace. Then, wheeling to the left, he blasted the ball all along the ground past five thunder-struck defenders.

I think if Sam were to look through his ITV sports film library he will see that it was a rolled rather than a blasted shot. I was never a blaster of the ball. I always envied the way players like Bobby Charlton, Peter Lorimer and Dave Mackay could hammer shots in from thirty yards. I couldn't burst a paper bag from a range of more than fifteen yards. This was one of the most satisfying goals of my career and it gave me particular pleasure because before the game started I had pledged to score a goal within five minutes.

Hardly pausing for breath at the end of an exhausting sea-son, I set off with the England squad for the World Cup Finals in Chile. We stopped off on the way in Peru, as Desmond Hackett reported in the *Daily Express* of 20 May 1962:

Jimmy Greaves, at his glorious best, scored a first-half hat-trick here against Peru to set England off to a goal-studded start as they head for the serious business of World Cup campaigning in Chile.

I remember that match for the fact that Bobby Moore made his England debut. He played with supreme confidence and was hardly out of the team from then on until his retirement a record 108 caps later. Bobby and I became constant com-panions and dedicated drinking partners. I could not have asked for a better side-kick. In private he is a warm and very humorous character and far from the cold, calculating image that he always projected on the football field where he had few peers.

My hat-trick and Bobby's controlled debut performance

provided the sportswriters with what proved to be just about the last chance to write anything favourable about the England team on that best-forgotten trip. Donald Saunders, a distinguished-looking Welshman, who reports boxing and football for the *Daily Telegraph*, made this summing-up after England had been beaten by Brazil in the quarter-finals in Chile:

A succession of victories in 1960–61 encouraged the growth of a tremendous team spirit in England's dressing-room. This began to wither in the autumn of 1961 and by June 1962 had disappeared. No one who had travelled with England on their summer tour of Portugal, Italy and Austria would have believed that, in Chile just twelve months later, some players could fairly be accused of not having their heart in the game. Everyone, it seemed, had been proud to wear an England shirt, was conscious of his responsibility and was determined to prove himself worthy of the honour. The following year, there were some men in the England party who wanted only to return home as quickly as possible ...

I am sure I was one of the players at whom Don was pointing an accusing finger and have to admit that while in Chile I got a bad attack of homesickness. I'd had a bellyful of foreign places after my nightmare in Milan and the punishing European Cup campaign with Spurs. By the time the World Cup came round my appetite for football had been blunted. It would not have been so bad had we been housed in comfort in Chile but we were stuck half way up a mountain in spartan living quarters and miles from any sort of sophisticated life. I hated every minute of it and frankly have to concede that I failed to perform at anything like my best in the World Cup matches. The 1962 World Cup was not one of my better experiences.

A family holiday helped restore my appetite and by the start of the following season I was raring to go again, as Bill Holden reported in the *Daily Mirror* of 11 August 1962:

Jimmy Greaves is going to be the game's biggest box-office draw this season because of his sheer goal-snatching flair. Jimmy hit two and helped with the other three as Spurs destroyed League champions Ipswich in the Charity Shield match at Portman Road.

A couple of weeks later I was giving that fine former amateur international football star Tony Pawson something to get quite excited about in *The Observer* of 25 August 1962:

At Upton Park there was murder most pleasant as Spurs destroyed West Ham with soccer that was a dream to watch, a nightmare to play against. The impish executioner inevitably was Greaves. This was the finest all-round performance I have seen from an English inside-forward. His dribbling had a magical unreality as the impossible was made to appear easy.

Alan Williams, a larger than life character in the Midlands who was for many years the Midlands 'Voice of Football' for the *Daily Express*, saw me in action at Molineux on 18 September 1962:

Jimmy Greaves plundered two of his most impish goals in five stunning minutes to transform this Molineux thriller and send Tottenham away from Wolverhampton with a proudly-earned point.

Ten days later, I was giving my 'rabbit' team Nottingham Forest another hiding as Bill Holden reported in the *Daily Mirror*:

Jimmy Greaves led Tottenham on an incredible nine-goal spree against Nottingham Forest, demonstrating his wide variety of scoring methods. He headed the first goal, calmly side-footed his second and fourth – and raced through to hit a tremendous drive on the run for his third.

I always looked forward to my games against Manchester United. They had an exciting atmosphere all their own and used to bring the best out of all the players. Clive Toye saw our match at White Hart Lane on 24 October 1962, when United were struggling to find their form. He told *Daily Express* readers the next morning:

Super Spurs looked Britain's answer to Santos, Brazil's world club champions, as they slapped £488,000 Manchester United to the bottom of the First Division last night. Leading the goal glut, of course, was Jimmy Greaves. He scored three and hit a post as Tottenham romped to a 6–2 triumph.

We were drawn against Glasgow Rangers in the second round of the European Cup Winners' Cup and the Press built it up into a match for the British club championship. Bill Holden was at the first leg at White Hart Lane on 29 October 1962, and wrote in the *Daily Mirror*:

Top honours in this 5–2 Spurs romp went to Jimmy Greaves, who showed the kind of fight and skill he does not always produce for England. Three of the goals against Rangers came from corner-kicks he took on the right wing and it was Greaves more than anyone who gave Spurs their supremacy over the Scots.

I always enjoyed playing against my old buddy Gordon Banks, the greatest of all England goalkeepers. We were good friends off the pitch but were always out to get the better of each other once we were in opposition in a match. It was never easy to put the ball past Gordon because he was a master of positioning and knew just when to leave his line to narrow the angle. I managed to find a way past him in a League match on 9 November 1962, as Alan Hoby reported in the *Sunday Express*:

Jimmy Greaves scored one of the greatest goals I have seen before 52,000 applauding spectators in the sunshine and joy of White Hart Lane yesterday. He did a swaying, dribbling ballet dance past four stupefied defenders. Then, drawing goalkeeper Gordon Banks out of goal with another effortless swerve, Greaves calmly placed the ball into the empty net. Everyone of us rose to applaud this wonderful solo effort.

A couple of weeks later, Walter Winterbottom had his final match as England team manager. I was very fond of Walter, a thoroughbred gentleman who was a fanatic about football tactics. Much of Walter's theory used to go way over my head but I respected his knowledge, even if I couldn't always grasp exactly what he was trying to tell me. It gave me a lot of pleasure to score the final goal of his England reign. This is how Clive Toye described it in the *Daily Express* of 21 November 1962:

Three minutes from the end of a soccer era, Jimmy Greaves ended the non-stop pounding of Wales with the sort of goal England begged from him in the heat of the World Cup six months ago. With the last minutes of Walter Winterbottom's reign as England team manager ticking away, Greaves dummied past four defenders to lash the ball left-footed into the net.

I still harboured grievances about the way some of my Milan team-mates had treated me during the Italian Affair and went out of my way to show them a thing or two about how the game should be played in an inter-League match at Highbury on 3 December 1962. Bill Holden was there for the *Daily Mirror*:

Jimmy Greaves, who flirted with the land of the sun and the lire but found that British was best for him, scored one and made the other two Football League goals in this satisfying 3–2 victory over the Italian League at Highbury. Greaves was the difference between the two teams and the Italians must be wishing they had made him happy in Milan. They had nobody in his class near goal ...

Ken Jones, cousin of our flying winger Cliff and himself a former professional, is now the respected sports columnist for the *Sunday Mirror*. He was a young, up-and-coming reporter on the *Daily Mirror* when he saw Tottenham's European Cup Winners' Cup second leg match against Rangers at Ibrox on 10 December 1962:

Jimmy Greaves, Spurs' ace goal-snatcher, tore the heart out of every fan who boasted the bold blue of Rangers with one moment of majesty at Ibrox Park. Greaves swept out of a tackle and then thrust through from the halfway line to hammer home the goal that virtually killed this European Cup Winners' Cup tie second leg. Make no mistake about it, that goal was the killer.

Brian James, one of the *Daily Mail's* team of highly talented writers, saw me help myself to a Christmas Day hat-trick against Ipswich:

A hat-trick by Jimmy Greaves in the final five minutes highlighted a towering display of courage and control by his team on the snow-dusted, tortured turf. Ipswich had nothing to compare with the icy magic of Greaves, White, Jones and Mackay.

A fine example of the descriptive writing skill of Brian James came in the *Daily Mail* of 15 April 1963, after we had smashed Liverpool 7–2:

> Like a king travelling incognito, with glimpses of majesty again and again shining through, Spurs moved a shade farther ahead of the common herd in the chase for the championship crown yesterday with this 7–2 victory against Liverpool. Jimmy Greaves provided a four-goal flourish as Tottenham topped a hundred League goals for the season.

I was sent off only once in my career as a Football League player, as Laurie Pignon reported in the *Daily Sketch* of 24 April 1963:

> With Jimmy Greaves sensationally sent off for the first time in his life, Spurs fought like ten Dave Mackays to snatch their greatest-ever overseas victory in the first leg of their European Cup Winners' Cup semi-final against OFK Belgrade here in Yugoslavia tonight.

It was one of the few times I had lost my temper on a football field. OFK had been ultra defensive and nasty with it. There were a lot of boots flying around and they were giving us plenty of stick. So Dave Mackay and Bobby Smith started to even things out a bit and I cannot think of two blokes I would rather have on my side in a rough-house. It was due to Smithy's enthusiasm – for the want of a better word – that I got sent for an early bath for the first time in my career. Going for a ball, his elbow caught their centre-half in the stomach. It really took the wind out of the bloke and he went down on his knees. I stood looking on quite innocently when suddenly this feller jumps up and comes at me like a bull. He wasn't a bad judge picking on little me, rather than the massive Smithy. Anyway, he threw a punch and missed and I immediately threw one back – and missed. I never was any good at counter punching. The Hungarian referee saw the whole incident but chose to pick on me. And with 70,000 Yugoslavs yelling blue murder, who could blame him! I could hardly believe it when he told me to go to the dressing-room. What hurt most of all was that I had not even had the satisfaction of making any contact with my attempted punch. The crowd were going mad, throwing bottles and abuse. Cliffie Jones, who had been sitting on the touchline bench, escorted me off the pitch with a protective arm around my shoulders. 'Come on, Jimbo,' he said, his eyes shining with excitement. 'I'll see you're all right. Let 'em all come at us. We can take 'em.' Cliffie's Welsh blood was boiling and he was enjoying every second of it. Me, I was frightened stiff.

We had the last laugh on OFK by beating them and going through to the European Cup Winners' Cup Final against Atletico Madrid in Rotterdam on 14 May 1963. This was how Ken Jones reported our memorable victory in the *Daily Mirror*:

Spurs won the European Cup Winners' Cup here in Rotterdam tonight with this five-goal massacre of Atletico Madrid and so became the first British club to carry off one of Europe's top soccer trophies. This was the night of the return to form of goal ace Jimmy Greaves who scored twice ...

Alf Ramsey was now in charge of the England team and we gave him a great start to his first close-season tour with a thumping 4–2 victory over Czechoslovakia who just a year earlier had been World Cup runners-up to Brazil. Peter Lorenzo wrote in the *Daily Herald* of 29 May 1963:

All the Czech sneers that English football, like the British Empire, was a thing of the past, were crushingly answered here in Bratislava. Four spanking goals – two by Jimmy Greaves, one each by Bobby Smith and Bobby Charlton – were impressive enough rebuke for the arrogant, unfounded charges laid by so many Czech critics before the start of this international match.

Back to the bread-and-butter business of League football, I was once again on the mark against Nottingham Forest. Pat

Collins, the father of London *Evening News* sports columnist Pat Collins, reported in *The People* of 31 August 1963:

The biggest difference between Tottenham and Forest was Jimmy Greaves. Only he, with his uncanny goal flair, could so dramatically change Tottenham's pedestrian performance into a solid 4–1 win. And only he could have scored such a cheeky hat-trick.

Harry Miller, now chief football reporter for the *Daily Mirror*, saw Spurs go top of the First Division on 1 October 1963:

Spurs soared to the top of the First Division table for the first time this season. They did it with a super show against Birmingham that included a hat-trick from Jimmy Greaves, his third of the season.

A game that stands out even in my poor memory is when England played the Rest of the World in a match to mark the Centenary of the Football Association. It was staged at Wembley on 23 October 1963, and this was how Brian James described it in the *Daily Mail*:

A century of English soccer has ended. It drew to a fitting close at Wembley with the last 90 minutes that saw skill and courage create an England victory against the Rest of the World to be taken and held proudly high. This, above all, was Jimmy Greaves's greatest match. The quick wit and quicker aim of the deft, little Londoner have never before been spurred by such zeal for combat. It was his goal four minutes from time that put the seal of triumph on this historic match that marked the FA Centenary.

That winning goal, a simple prod after a Bobby Charlton blockbuster had been pushed out by Yugoslav goalkeeper Soskic, was consolation for having had as good a goal as I have ever scored ruled out. I survived a trip on my way past four defenders before slotting the ball into the net. My delight at having taken a star-studded defence apart was short-lived because Scottish referee Bobby Davidson had awarded England a free-kick for that trip. He later apologised for not playing the advantage rule. The Rest of the World squad, they used five substitutes, included players of the quality of Lev Yashin (Russia), Djalma Santos (Brazil), Puskas and di Stefano (Spain), Eusebio (Portugal), Kopa (France), Seeler (West Germany), Jim Baxter and Denis Law (Scotland). All the players who took part were each presented with an inscribed gold watch. I gave mine to my Dad. The honour of playing in the game was sufficient reward for me.

The following month I was in the England team that thrashed Northern Ireland 8–3 at Wembley. Ken Jones was there for the *Daily Mirror*:

England, a ruthless, goal-hungry England, rubbed the face of Irish football into the green turf of Wembley. Four goals by Jimmy Greaves and a Terry Paine hat-trick are the jewels that will sparkle in the memory.

Joe Hulme, who knew a thing or two about putting the ball into the net as a pre-war star with Arsenal and Huddersfield, reported in *The People* of 11 January 1964:

The lethal finishing of Jimmy Greaves put Spurs on top of the First Division. Greaves was the match-winner against Blackburn with a hat-trick that was Jimmy at his immaculate best.

John Bromley, now Head of Sport at London Weekend Television, was the *Daily Mirror* reporter in Copenhagen on 20 May 1964:

Jimmy Greaves, the goal maestro from Spurs, scored twice for the Rest of Europe team against Scandinavia here in Copenhagen to delight a 45,000 crowd. Helmut Schoen, the German manager of the European team for this showpiece match, said later: 'I thought Greaves was magnificent. He is certainly one of the finest players in Europe.'

My old pal Desmond Hackett got quite carried away in the *Daily Express* of 2 September 1964:

The author of Tottenham's 4–1 win against Burnley was Jim 'The Genius' Greaves. I have seldom seen him play with such skill, such industry and such admirable effect. This was world-class soccer at its peak. What an England captain Greaves would make in this wondrous mood!

That captaincy comment must have made Alf Ramsey choke on his cornflakes. I had as much chance being made England captain as climbing Mount Everest. Alf would have been too worried that I would have led the players into too many bars. Sorry, Des, but I was much too much of an individualist to have been trusted with the captaincy of any team.

Joe Hulme saw me score my hundredth goal for Spurs. He reported in *The People* on 19 September 1964:

Jimmy Greaves was back at his magnificent goal-grabbing best to spark Tottenham's fifth successive home victory. He scored the only goal of the game – his hundredth League goal for Spurs – and might have finished with five but for a super display by West Brom goalkeeper Ray Potter.

Frank Butler, Sports Editor of the *News of the World* and a walking record book on boxing, thought England were out for the count against Northern Ireland in Belfast. But we came from behind for a knockout victory, as Frank reported on 3 October 1964:

Jimmy Greaves saved the pride of English soccer its biggest humiliation for 37 years. It was that many years ago that Ireland last beat England in Belfast. Without the aid of a fantastic Greaves hat-trick in 11 minutes Ireland would have won. This swift haul gave Greaves a new English international scoring record of 35 goals – two more than Bobby Charlton.

We had been trailing 3–1 with 15 minutes to go and as a young, snake-hipped winger called George Best, making his first appearance against England, tormented our defence, I thought to myself, 'Aye, aye ... he's going to give us trouble for years to come...'

In the past we had always tended to dismiss Holland as an inferior footballing nation but there were the first clear signs that they were emerging as a power in world soccer when we struggled to a 1–1 draw against them in Amsterdam, as

Frank McGhee reported in the *Daily Mirror* on 10 December 1964:

> Jimmy Greaves, the deadliest goal thief in the business, has scored more times for England than any other player. But even he has not scored one so desperately needed as the goal that silenced the Dutch crowd's excited song of victory in the Olympic Stadium here in Amsterdam.

Torquay United gave Tottenham a scare in the FA Cup and took us to a replay at White Hart Lane where Roy Peskett was on duty for the *Daily Mail* on 17 January 1965:

> Torquay's fans returned to Devon talking about Jimmy Greaves, the goal magician. Jimmy missed three chances in this FA Cup replay but also scored a hat-trick that sent brave Torquay crashing.

Ten days later I scored another hat-trick as my partnership with the elegant Alan Gilzean started to flourish. Malcolm Gunn wrote in the *News of the World*:

> Ipswich were demolished by the £170,000 firm of messrs. Greaves and Gilzean, goal contractors extraordinary. Greaves scored three and Gilzean two in what was a White Hart Lane walk-over.

I was never one for goal statistics. All I worried about was where the *next* goal was coming from. But there was always an army of helpful people, most of them in Fleet Street, ready to record my milestones. Bill Holden recorded in the *Daily Mirror* of 14 February 1965:

> It took Jimmy Greaves only 75 seconds to complete his personal record of getting a goal against every club currently in the First Division. Sheffield United were the only team he had never scored against.

A victory against the Scots is what all English footballers enjoy most. At Wembley on 9 April 1965, we were more than happy to salvage a draw, as Frank Butler reported in the *News of the World*:

> They still talk about the Wembley Wizards of 1928 – those wee

Blue Devils who trounced England 5–1 just thirty-seven years ago. Now it is the Wembley Warriors of 1965. For never has an England team with only nine fit men fought so bravely against such heavy odds. Bobby Charlton and Jimmy Greaves scored England's goals in a courage-carved draw against Scotland.

Norman Giller, who describes himself as the Original Ghost-writer of Fleet Street because of his Oxfam physique, was a football reporter with the *Daily Express* when he saw Tottenham take Blackburn Rovers apart at White Hart Lane on 14 April 1965:

Three goals from Alan Gilzean and two from Jimmy Greaves against Blackburn tell their own story of another slaughter by the mighty G-men of Tottenham. This was Gilzean's first three-goal haul for Spurs – but it could not rob Greaves of the man-of-the-match rating.

Alf Ramsey had something of a complex about Hungary, not surprising I suppose as his final international appearance for England was in the historic 6–3 drubbing of 1953. He was well pleased with our 1–0 win over the Hungarians at Wembley on 4 May 1965. Mind you, Desmond Hackett was not too impressed in the *Daily Express*:

England ended the 12-year mastery of Hungary at Wembley yesterday on the pitch where the famed magical Magyars whipped us 6–3 back in 1953. But, alas, there was little in this 1–0 victory to gloat about. The forward-line was an ever-increasing headache for Alf Ramsey. Only Jimmy Greaves can look back on the game with pride. He snatched the only goal of a mediocre game after 15 minutes.

Maurice Smith was a lovely bloke who reported football for *The People* for many years. I got to know Maurice well during his frequent trips to Milan when I was the 'little boy lost' in Italy. We found we had something in common away from football and that was a love for growing roses. I was a novice compared with Maurice, a green-fingered gardener who had quite a reputation as a rose grower. He used to advise me on gardening and there are several gardens in Essex that still display the Greaves roses. All of which brings me to this report by Maurice of 16 October 1965:

The ring-leader of Tottenham's 5–1 victory against Manchester United was Jimmy Greaves – back in the act as Lord Jim. Flooding out a tide of defence-splitting passes, he made the way for the first two goals and snatched the third after beating four men inside the space of his own hall carpet.

Maurice was also quite flowery when it came to writing! Steve Richards is a PR executive these days with Pepsi-Cola in New York, with special responsibilities for Pele and the Pepsi world youth football programme. On 26 October 1965, he was reporting for *The Sun* at White Hart Lane:

Jimmy Greaves has done it again! This incredible little man many would like to see axed by England twice burgled West Brom's defence to win a match even the most partisan Tottenham fan would admit Albion deserved to save.

Shortly after this game I went down with hepatitis and was out of action for three months. But it was more than a year before I shook off the after-effects of the illness. Reg Drury, a person I respect as a football reporter and like as a companion, saw my comeback match and wrote in the *News of the World* of 29 January 1966:

Jimmy Greaves is back in business. He got a hero's welcome at White Hart Lane and, after taking a jaundiced view of soccer during three months of inactivity, returned with a goal in the 4–0 hammering of Blackburn.

I worked desperately hard to get myself fit for England's 1966 World Cup challenge. People who considered that I was not interested in playing for my country obviously did not know that I had a burning ambition to help England win the World Cup. Desmond Hackett, Brian James and Peter Lorenzo, all reporters who had followed my footballing fortunes around the world, knew just how keen I was:

Jimmy Greaves played his way into England's World Cup squad

with one of the greatest shows I have ever seen from this brilliant but unpredictable player. Greaves, who had missed the last five international matches because of illness, was always in menacing action and was leaping for joy in celebration of a typical goal in the tenth minute of this match against Yugoslavia.

– Desmond Hackett, *Daily Express*, 4 May 1966

In crushing Norway 6–1 here in Oslo, England found the aggression of purpose, accuracy of shots and the honest professional heart I feared they lack. Jimmy Greaves, the man whose mission it is to score telling goals, took four off a team too good ever to be patronized.

– Brian James, *Daily Mail*, 28 June 1966

Jimmy Greaves was presented with a silver salver by the Danes to mark his fiftieth game for England here in Copenhagen. The thousands who came expecting to see a repeat of Jimmy's four-goal fireworks against Norway in Oslo were disappointed. Yet even in docile mood there was ever the hallmark of a world-class craftsman, as witness his opportunism that led to England's second goal.'

– Peter Lorenzo, *The Sun*, 3 July 1966

My scrapbooks are remarkably empty of any reference to the 1966 World Cup Finals. Let's face it, I didn't achieve anything worth writing about. That was the most disappointing period of my footballing life. I was glad to get back into action the following season when every goal I scored was my answer to the people who thought Alf Ramsey was right to leave me out of the World Cup Final team. Victor Railton saw me score two early-season goals against Tottenham's arch rivals Arsenal and reported in the *Evening News* of 2 September 1966:

Arsenal's unbeaten run ended at White Hart Lane this afternoon when they went down to slick Spurs. Cliff Jones gave Tottenham a first-half lead and Jimmy Greaves neatly found the net in the fifty-seventh and sixty-ninth minutes to prove he remains the best goal poacher in the business.

Inter-League matches seem to have gone out of fashion now. I played in one of the last of these prestige games in

Dublin on 8 November 1967, when the Football League beat the League of Ireland 7–2. This was how Laurie Pignon reported it in the *Daily Sketch*:

Jimmy Greaves set up the Irish for slaughter last night with a goal that demonstrated his anxiety for an England recall. Greaves, playing with all his old enthusiasm and efficiency, sparked a first-half five-goal spree with a sizzling shot from 15 yards.

There were rumours that Spurs were preparing to sell me after Bill Nick had left me out of the first-team a couple of times midway through the 1967–8 season but Bill squashed the talk by recalling me for the fourth round FA Cup tie against Preston. Steve Richards reported in *The Sun* of 19 February 1968:

Jimmy Greaves, the master executioner, gave a two-goal answer to those people who thought he had lost his scoring appetite. He knocked Preston out of the FA Cup to finally kill off talk that Spurs would even consider parting with one of the game's true artists.

I was never a great fan of the way Leeds played football under the direction of Don Revie. They were certainly effective but their win-at-all-costs methods left a lot to be desired. It was always satisfying to be on the winning side against them, particularly when we ended one of their long unbeaten runs at White Hart Lane on 12 April 1968. Peter 'The Poet' Batt, one of the great characters of Fleet Street and now twinkling on the *Daily Star*, was then reporting for *The Sun*:

Leeds, the team that had forgotten how to lose, yesterday received a rude reminder from Spurs about the despair of defeat. It was their first set-back in 27 matches and, almost inevitably, it was that genius of a goal scorer Jimmy Greaves who conjured up the winning goal.

Peter Corrigan, these days Sports Editor of *The Observer*, was writing for the *Daily Mail* when he saw Spurs take Burnley apart at White Hart Lane on 6 September 1968:

It is like welcoming back an old friend to see Jimmy Greaves thieving goals with his old panache. He helped himself to a hat-trick and created three other goals in this 7–0 blitz of Burnley.

People often ask me what is the greatest goal I ever scored. I have a stock answer, 'The next one.' It seems I impressed Bill Nicholson with one of my goals against Leicester City, as Brian Scovell reported in the *Daily Sketch* on 6 October 1968:

Manager Bill Nicholson described the first of Jimmy Greaves's three goals against Leicester as possibly the greatest he has ever scored. He collected a clearance from Pat Jennings, beat four men in a 30-yard run and finished it with a perfectly-placed left foot shot.

I've never been one to get excited about goals. I am just happy as long as they go into the net. It doesn't matter how they get there as long as they count as goals. Cheeky goals always give me a lot of satisfaction, such as the one Harry Miller described in the *Daily Mirror* of 19 October 1968:

Liverpool's defenders had eyes only for Terry Venables as he feigned anger at the positioning of their defensive wall. Greaves stepped up unnoticed and cheekily curled his 199th First Division goal for Tottenham into the net.

Dear old Vic Railton kept plugging for me to return to the England attack, even though there was little chance of Sir Alf recalling me. He wrote in the *Evening News* of 16 November 1968:

Jimmy Greaves snatched four goals in this 5–1 slamming of Sunderland. How much longer can England afford to ignore the claims of Britain's top hot-shot?

Desmond Hackett saw me score the two goals that put Spurs through to the sixth round of the FA Cup. He reported in the *Daily Express* of 12 February 1969:

Rejected by goal-bankrupt England, Jimmy Greaves scored twice to put Tottenham into the sixth round of the FA Cup last night at the expense of Tommy Docherty's Aston Villa braves.

Early in the following season, I reached another milestone

with Spurs, as Bob Ferrier reported in the *Sunday Express* of 30 August 1969:

A peerless, vintage goal to crown a great occasion. It came from the one and only Jimmy Greaves as he celebrated his 300th League game for Spurs. He found the Ipswich net with an incredible overhead flick with his left foot.

Little did I know it but this was to be my last season with my beloved Spurs. One of my last goals for them almost got even me excited. This is how Peter Corrigan described it in the *Daily Mail* on 18 October 1969:

It was a goal fashioned out of nothing. Greaves collected the ball five yards inside his own half and then set off on an extraordinary 60-yard gallop at the end of which the ball was tucked into the back of the Newcastle net and a queue of beaten defenders were left fighting for breath.

At the end of the year – and the decade – the *Daily Express* conducted a poll among the League managers:

Jimmy Greaves has been voted the top striker of the Sixties by the managers who were in power during the greatest decade in the history of English football. Greaves pipped Geoff Hurst, with Francis Lee edging Denis Law into fourth place.

But it was obvious I was not going to figure very prominently in the 1970s. By the time the transfer deadline came around in March I had been lined up for a move to West Ham as makeweight in a deal that took Martin Peters to Tottenham. Alan Hoby reported my West Ham debut for the *Sunday Express* on 20 March 1970:

Jimmy Greaves – greatest goalscorer of our time, perhaps of all time – has done it again. In a bizarre and fantastic game against Manchester City, our Jim launched West Ham to their biggest win of the season with two typical cool and cheeky goals. He has now scored in all his major debuts.

Little went right for me at West Ham after that great send-off and the Blackpool nightclub affair on New Year's Day, 1971, convinced me that I was in my last season as a League footballer. Bernard Joy reported in the *Evening Standard* of 9 February 1971:

With the goal that defeated Coventry, West Ham and former England ace scorer Jimmy Greaves began his reparations for the Blackpool escapade which led to the disciplining of Bobby Moore, Brian Dear, Clyde Best and himself. It was his 353rd League goal and one of his most valuable, considerably easing West Ham's fears of relegation.

Norman Giller saw me score my last goal in League football. He wrote in the *Daily Express* of 9 April 1971:

The Jimmy Greaves gift for scoring the goals that count has rarely been more gratefully accepted than by West Ham at Upton Park. Greaves, as nimble as a thimble, stitched this game up for Hammers five minutes from the end to leave West Bromwich Albion dazed. He steered the ball home from a tight angle after a Brooking shot had been blocked.

And that was that. The final entry in my scrapbooks. I hope I have not been too self-indulgent with this sentimental journey into my past. After suffering through five lost years, it is rewarding to have printed proof that I have achieved something during my lifetime. My grateful thanks to the football writers who helped record it all.

Like I was saying a few thousand words ago, it wasn't all drinking.

10

The revolution

'What has gone from the game
– I suspect irretrievably – is fun.'
– Geoffrey Green (*The Times*)

My playing career bridged two worlds. When I first came into League football as a seventeen-year-old debutant with Chelsea my weekly wage was £4–10s (£4.50). Senior professionals were earning £17 in the season and £14 in the summer. That was in 1957. A year later the maximum wage was lifted to £20 a week. There was an incentive bonus of £4 for a win and £2 for a draw. These were the days of 'Slave Soccer'.

Under threat of strike action by the Professional Footballers' Association eloquently led by Jimmy Hill and Cliff Lloyd, the Football League bosses did a startling turnabout and agreed to a no-ceiling wage structure that revolutionised football almost overnight.

It seems astonishing in these inflationary times when £10,000 a year footballers are commonplace to think that when I made my England debut against Peru in 1959 I was earning just £20 a week. International fees per match then were £50, a figure that had risen only £10 by the time I played my final game for England in 1967.

The revolution was not confined to the wage packet. It was even more sweeping on the pitch where the tactical side of the game changed out of sight. My first and last England matches illustrate the point I am making.

Against Peru in Lima in 1959 we lined up in 2–3–5 formation, with two wingers playing wide on the flanks:

HOPKINSON
HOWE   ARMFIELD
CLAYTON   WRIGHT   FLOWERS
DEELEY GREAVES CHARLTON(R) HAYNES HOLDEN

In my final England appearance against Austria in Vienna in 1967 the line-up was a cautious and restrictive 4–3–3:

BONETTI
NEWTON   LABONE   MOORE   WILSON
MULLERY   BALL   HUNTER
GREAVES   HURST   HUNT

I was happiest in the 2–3–5 days when the accent was on attack and before the game became hooked on the drug of defensive football. There has been a refreshing move towards more open football in the last couple of seasons but today's top teams are still a long way short of providing the sort of entertainment that was part and parcel of the game when I was a young £20-a-week professional.

The game started to go sick in the mid-1960s. This was when the 'Fear Factor' took a grip at all levels. Everyone was suddenly frightened of failure. The *manager* because his job was in danger. The *player* because he could lose his first-team place and the bonus money that went with it. The *director* desperate to cling on to his boardroom place which gave him upmanship over his business associates. The *fan* because of the 'stick' he had to take from workmates if the team with which he was identified lost.

You could almost reach out and feel the pressure and tension at First Division matches. It even got to Tottenham's Bill Nicholson who had always been an advocate of open, free-expression football. He started to go against his principles and followed the trend towards formations geared to stopping rather than scoring goals.

In the year that Spurs performed the League and FA Cup double, they scored 115 First Division goals and conceded 55. In my last full season at White Hart Lane they scored 54 and conceded 55. We were all running scared. Don't tell me the game has changed for the better.

My remedy for relieving the pressure was to take refuge in the bar-room after every match.

It was at international level that I witnessed the most revolutionary changes during my career. When I made my debut, the England side was picked by a team of selectors with Walter Winterbottom responsible for the coaching and management. It was an amateurish set-up and I often used to wonder if some of the selectors knew the first thing about football.

Most of them were elderly gentlemen, old enough to be grandfathers of the players they were selecting. They used to unconsciously give us hours of amusement with their behaviour on overseas tours. I have often seen them nodding off at the dinner table at after-match banquets and several of them seemed to have the booze problem that was later to cause me so much trouble. On one tour I recall one of the old boys praising the performance of Ron Flowers after a match that Ron had watched from the touchline bench. They were all well-meaning people who devoted hours to football as a hobby. But the international arena is no place for amateurs. The Football Association have become more enterprising and efficient in their approach to the game but ideally I would still like to see football in the hands of the professionals with no interference from amateurs.

Alf Ramsey took the England managership in succession to Walter Winterbottom only on condition that he had the sole right to pick the team. I played 25 matches under Walter, of which 12 were won, eight lost and five drawn. With Alf, I played in 32 internationals, finishing on the winning side 18 times with six defeats and eight draws.

There was a lot of chopping, and changing – much of it need-less – when the selectors were responsible for picking the team, while Alf tried to stick to a settled squad. He often ignored club form because he knew that players respond differently to the challenge of international football.

Alf inherited a 4–2–4 set-up from Walter in which Johnny Haynes had been the keyman with his precision passing from a midfield base. But Johnny's international career was wrecked by a car smash before Alf took over and it took him some time before he got a midfield set-up that satisfied him. Finally he settled for a 4–3–3 formation, playing sometimes with just one winger and then with no winger at all. Alf was simply playing to England's strength at the time and I am sure it was not his intention to wipe wingers off the face of football. But England's triumph in winning the World Cup in 1966 spawned an army of imitators and suddenly everybody was playing the 4–3–3 way with the emphasis heavily on defence.

I speak from painful memory when I say that it made life much harder for goal scorers. Penalty areas were suddenly as packed as Piccadilly in the rush hour and goals, the lifeblood of the game, began to be in short supply. New phrases started to creep into the language of the game. Work-rate . . . the over-lap . . . tackling back . . . running off the ball . . . ball watching. When I first came into the game I was an inside-forward, pure and simple. By the mid-1960s I was known as a striker.

It has never been a secret that I am anti-coaching. I am firmly of the opinion that many coaches have done more harm than good to English football. They stifle the natural instincts of players and turn them into robots. Our football until recently had become so stereotyped that it was difficult to tell one team from another. Great individualists had almost disappeared from the game and for that I blame the coaches.

The good news is that the game is at last coming out of a long dark tunnel. Wingers are on the way back thanks to the emergence of players like Peter Barnes, Steve Coppell, Gordon

Hill, John Robertson and Clive Woods. And I think the 'Black Explosion' can only help the game. The rise of black stars like Cyrille Regis, Laurie Cunningham, Viv Anderson, Bob Hazell, Roger Palmer, Vince Hilaire and Luther Blissett has given League football a lift.

I applauded Tottenham's vision and courage in signing Argentinian World Cup stars Osvaldo Ardiles and Ricardo Villa. Irrespective of whether the double deal was rewarded with a major trophy, it showed the sort of thinking and action needed to steer our game out of the straitjacket into which it had been placed by our coaches.

Mind you, the League must be careful not to allow wholesale import of foreign players. This would cramp the progress of young footballers who are just starting out on their careers and need the incentive of a possible first-team place as their goal. I speak with feeling on this subject because my fifteen-year-old son, Danny – named after his Godfather Danny Blanchflower – is a junior on Tottenham's books.

I hope he reads this book and learns from his father's mistakes.

There is a selector lurking in every one of us and I am no exception. Norman Giller, the journalist who has helped me get my thoughts down on paper, has worked it out that I played with 74 different players while winning my 57 England caps. The following statistics are his and the comments mine as I try to pick the best England team from the list. The figures following each name show the number of times I played with them in the England side ...

GOALKEEPERS
Gordon Banks 20 (W12 L3 D5); Peter Bonetti 3 (W3);
Alan Hodgkinson 1 (W); Eddie Hopkinson 5 (W1 D1 L3);
Ron Springett 24 (W12 L7 D5); Tony Waiters 4 (W1 L1 D2).

I have no hesitation in picking Gordon Banks as the greatest of the England goalkeepers that I played with. There was not a weakness in his game. He was a master at positional play, his handling was superb, his reflexes remarkable and he had a controlled temperament that helped steady the players around him in moments of crisis. Banksie was always the boss of his goal area and never let anybody forget it. He often used to bawl defensive team-mates out if they fell below the perfection standards that he set.

We used to call Gordon 'Fernandel' because of his likeness to the great French comic and he had a marvellous sense of humour to go with his looks. We used to have talking matches when we played against each other. If he saved one of my shots he would call, 'You'll have to do better than that, Greavsie.' Sometimes when taking the ball towards him I would point to where I was going to put my shot and if and when I tucked it past him into the net I would say, 'Pick that one out.'

Whenever Gordon and I get together we still laugh over a goal I scored against him during his days at Leicester. Tottenham were murdering them by about three goals to nothing when we were awarded a penalty late in the game. As I bent down to put the ball on the spot I noticed Gordon going through his usual pre-penalty ritual of spitting on his hands and reaching for a post to get his distance. He had his left arm stretched out and was looking at the post when, still crouched at the penalty spot, I rolled the ball ever so gently with my left foot into the opposite corner of the net. I fully expected the kick to be taken again but went through the pretence of exaggerated celebrations, kissing and cuddling my team-mates. I don't know who was more shocked, Gordon or me, when the ref awarded a goal!

Anyway, Gordon was for me the king of all goalkeepers.

FULL BACKS
Tony Allen 2 (L1 D1); John Angus 1 (L);
Jimmy Armfield 31 (W17 L9 D5); Gerry Byrne 2 (W1 L1);
George Cohen 19 (W10 L3 D6); Ron Henry 1 (L);
Don Howe 5 (W1 L3 D1); Mick McNeill 8 (W7 D1);
Keith Newton 2 (W2); Graham Shaw 1 (W);

Ken Shellito 1 (W); Bobby Thomson 6 (W2 L1 D3);
Ray Wilson 35 (W18 L8 D9).

Ray Wilson walks into the left-back position. He was one of the most accomplished full-backs I ever played with or against. Ray was a beautiful stylist, always properly balanced and a fine striker of the ball. He could keep pace with the fastest wingers, had quick recovery powers and tackled with the full weight of his body. The perfect full-back. Ray had a rascal's sense of humour and was the man behind many leg pulls. It's difficult to imagine him in his new profession as an undertaker. Excuse the pun, Ray, but you could make me die laughing! Thinking back over past conversations I now begin to wonder what you used to mean when you described me as good in the box.

It is much more difficult to select a right-back partner for Wilson. Jimmy Armfield, George Cohen and Don Howe were all superb players and Ken Shellito, my old Chelsea buddy, would have been up there with the best of them but for a knee injury bringing a premature end to his career. After a lot of thought, I finally plump for Armfield who to my mind was the man who invented the overlap. He was quick, expert at positioning and always tried to use the ball intelligently. Jimmy just gets my vote over George Cohen, who was a great-hearted competitor but occasionally careless with his crosses after making marvellous runs down the right wing.

CENTRE BACKS
Jack Charlton 12 (W6 L2 D4); Ron Flowers 32 (W15 L10 D7);
Norman Hunter 2 (W2); Brian Labone 5 (W4 L1);
Bobby Moore 38 (W21 L8 D9); Maurice Norman 20
(W9 L5 D6);
Trevor Smith 2 (L1 D1); Peter Swan 11 (W7 L2 D2);
Billy Wright 3 (W1 L2).

The only problem I have here is which player to put alongside Bobby Moore, who is an automatic choice. He is the greatest defender I have ever seen, composed and commanding under the severest pressure. His critics – mostly north of Watford – always argued that he lacked pace and was not the greatest header of a ball known to man. Both are fair points but he was such a master reader of the game that he always knew exactly the right place to be to give the least possibility of progress for the man he was marking. And there was nobody better than Bobby when it came to distribution. His long passes from out of defence were always designed to trigger a counter attack. He was ice cool and a quick thinker who led by example. His standards were so high that everybody around him was inspired to lift their game. He was also a marvellous drinking partner. Cheers, Bobby!

I will not include Billy Wright in the running for the no. 5 shirt. Billy and I played with each other only in the last three of his 105 international matches when he was on the wind-down to the end of his glorious career. So it is difficult for me to judge him fairly. It's a three-man race between the raw power of Maurice Norman, the all-round ability of Peter Swan and the inelegant but effective drive of Jack Charlton.

Jack wins it, dare I say, by a neck from Swan and Norman both of whom did a sound job when on international duty. One of my saddest days in football was when I heard that Peter had got himself mixed up in the bribery scandal that led to his expulsion from the game. It was completely out of character for a man whom I liked and respected both as a player and as a person. Knowing he was of previous good character, I would have given him only a temporary ban from the game as a lesson. Jack Charlton gets the edge over Swan and Norman because of his ability for snatching vital goals.

THE MIDFIELD

Stan Anderson 1 (L); Alan Ball 7 (W4 L1 D2);
Bobby Charlton 47 (W25 L14 D8); Ron Clayton 6 (W1 L3 D2);
Chris Crowe 1 (D); George Eastham 12 (W9 L2 D1);
Ron Flowers 32 (W15 L10 D7); Johnny Haynes 20 (W10 L7 D3);

Freddie Hill 2 (W2); John Hollins 1 (W);
Tony Kay 1 (W); Wilf McGuinness 1 (L);
Jimmy Melia 2 (W1 L1); Brian Miller 1 (L);
Gordon Milne 11 (W8 L2 D1); Alan Mullery 2 (W2);
Martin Peters 5 (W4 L1); Bobby Robson 10 (W8 L1 D1);
Nobby Stiles 12 (W6 L2 D4); Terry Venables 2 (D2).

From this wealth of talent I have to pick just two players for my two midfield prongs in my 4–2–4 formation team. You will have noticed that I have included Ron Flowers as a midfield player as well as with the centre-backs. This strong and dependable player who gave such splendid service to Wolves was equally effective as a defender or coming forward from midfield.

Despite the strong claims of skilful artists like George Eastham, Martin Peters, Alan Ball and Terry Venables, I am plumping for pass master Johnny Haynes as the chief midfield marshall. There was nobody to touch him for providing the long positive pass that could take any defence apart and make the job of the goal scorers so much easier.

As his midfield partner I have to choose between the elegance and style of Bobby Robson, the competitive drive and ball-winning ability of Nobby Stiles or the combination of skill and power of Alan Mullery. My vote goes to Robson because he had goal scoring flair and clear in my mind is the memory of a procession of fine performances he gave while in harness with Haynes both for Fulham and England.

What, no Bobby Charlton? He is waiting in the wings ...

THE WINGERS
Peter Brabrook 1 (L); Warren Bradley 2 (L1 W1);
Ian Callaghan 1 (W); Bobby Charlton 47 (W25 L14 D8);
John Connelly 12 (W5 L3 D4); Norman Deeley 1 (L);
Bryan Douglas 18 (W9 L5 D4); Mike Hellawell 2 (W1 D1);
Alan Hinton 2 (D2); Doug Holden 2 (L2);
Ed Holliday 1 (L); Mike O'Grady 1 (W);
Terry Paine 14 (W10 L1 D3); Bobby Tambling 3 (W2 L1);
Peter Thompson 9 (W3 L2 D4).

For my team, I would insist on having two wingers. On the right I would have the darting, dangerous Bryan Douglas who was almost in the Stanley Matthews class as an outside-right. Over on the left would be Bobby Charlton, who was possibly more effective for England in his midfield role but was at his most explosive in his early days as a winger with a blitzing shot. Bobby could drop back into midfield to give assistance to Haynes and Robson if needed, which reminds me that Bryan Douglas was also a first-rate deep-lying inside-forward for Blackburn when the occasion demanded.

THE STRIKERS
Joe Baker 2 (L1 D1); Barry Bridges 4 (W1 L1 D2);
Johnny Byrne 8 (W4 L2 D2); Ray Charnley 1 (D);
Brian Clough 2 (L1 D1); Jimmy Greaves 57 (W30 L14 D13);
Gerry Hitchens 6 (W3 L3); Roger Hunt 8 (W6 D2);
Geoff Hurst 5 (W4 L1); Derek Kevan 2 (W1 L1);
Alan Peacock 5 (W3 D2); Fred Pickering 2 (W1 D1);
Bobby Smith 15 (W9 L4 D2); Frank Wignall 1 (D).

I shall selfishly claim one of the two central striking positions for myself as I am the sole selector and it is no race as to which player I shall pick as my plundering partner. Despite the powerful presence of great players like Geoff Hurst, Johnny Byrne, Roger Hunt, Brian Clough and Gerry Hitchens, I have no hesitation in selecting Bobby Smith.

I always considered Bobby the perfect foil for me. He had the strength and tenacity of two men, could win the ball on the ground or in the air and was a master at laying the ball off to team-mates either side of him. And he was also no slouch when it came to thumping the ball into the net himself. I fed off Bobby for years and feel he never received the credit he deserved. He was probably the best England centre-forward since Tommy Lawton.

So this is how my dream team would look:

BANKS

ARMFIELD   CHARLTON (J)   MOORE   WILSON

ROBSON   HAYNES

DOUGLAS   GREAVES   SMITH   CHARLTON (R)

As substitute I will go for the fiercely competitive Nobby
Stiles. It would make our opponents shudder to see him sitting
on the touchline straining to get into the action.

And how about this for my shadow side:

SPRINGETT

COHEN   SWAN   HUNTER   MCNEILL

MULLERY   EASTHAM

PAINE   HUNT   HURST   THOMPSON

Substitute: The elegant Martin Peters, with the ability to
slot in anywhere.

And could you beat this for a reserve reserve side?

BONETTI

HOWE   NORMAN   FLOWERS   NEWTON

BALL   VENABLES

CALLAGHAN   CLOUGH   BYRNE   CONNELLY

Substitute: Gordon Milne, who might be needed to win the
ball in midfield.

After studying this list of players which reads like a who's
who of English football, I feel proud and privileged to have
played with so many outstanding players. Believe me, it's quite
a sobering thought!

*Thanks for staying with me to the end
and remember, this one's on me.*

Appendix 1

The Greaves gallery of goals

A statistical study of his scoring record compiled by
Norman Giller

Jimmy Greaves played in 516 Football League matches and scored 357 goals, all of them in the First Division:

CHELSEA   124 (1957–61)
TOTTENHAM   220 (1961–70)
WEST HAM   13 (1970–71)

His average score per First Division game was .691 and he was leading First Division goal scorer a record six times:

1958–59 (32), 1960–61 (41), 1962–63 (37)
1963–64 (35), 1964–65 (29), 1968–69 (27)

These are the teams against which he scored his goals:

NOTTINGHAM FOREST (24), BURNLEY (19),
BIRMINGHAM CITY (17), BLACKPOOL (18),
WEST BROMWICH ALBION (16), WOLVES (17),
LEICESTER CITY (15), MANCHESTER CITY (15),
WEST HAM UNITED (16), BLACKBURN ROVERS (14),
MANCHESTER UNITED (13), NEWCASTLE UNITED (13),
FULHAM (12), ARSENAL (11), ASTON VILLA (11),
EVERTON (11), LIVERPOOL (11), LEEDS UNITED (10),

PRESTON NORTH END (10), SHEFFIELD UNITED (9),
SUNDERLAND (10), IPSWICH TOWN (9),
SHEFFIELD WEDNESDAY (8), STOKE CITY (7),
SOUTHAMPTON (6), BOLTON WANDERERS (5),
COVENTRY CITY (5), PORTSMOUTH (5),
TOTTENHAM HOTSPUR (5), CHELSEA (4),
CARDIFF CITY (2), DERBY COUNTY (2),
LUTON TOWN (2), NORTHAMPTON TOWN (1),
ORIENT (1), QUEEN'S PARK RANGERS (1).

He was top scorer for his club in 12 of the 14 seasons in which he played in the First Division.

Jimmy scored three or more goals in 22 First Division matches:

FOR CHELSEA – 4 v. Portsmouth (57–58); 3 v. Sheffield Wednesday (57–58); 5 v. Wolves (58–59); 3 v. Nottingham Forest (58–59); 3 v. Preston (59–60); 3 v. Birmingham City (59–60); 5 v. Preston (59–60); 3 v. Wolves (60–61); 3 v. Blackburn (60–61); 3 v. Manchester City (60–61); 5 v. West Bromwich Albion (60–61); 4 v. Newcastle United (60–61); 4 v. Nottingham Forest (60–61).

FOR SPURS – 3 v. Blackpool (61–62); 4 v. Nottingham Forest (62–63); 3 v. Manchester United (62–63); 3 v. Ipswich Town (62–63); 4 v. Liverpool (62–63); 3 v. Nottingham Forest (63–64); 3 v. Blackpool (63–64); 3 v. Birmingham City (63–64); 3 v. Blackburn Rovers (63–64).

He scored 35 goals in the FA Cup:

FOR CHELSEA – 1 v. Newcastle (58–59); 1 v. Aston Villa (58–59); 1 v. Bradford (59–60).

FOR SPURS – 3 v. Birmingham City (61–62); 2 v. Plymouth (61–62); 2 v. West Bromwich Albion (61–62); 1 v. Manchester United (semi-final, 61–62); 1 v. Burnley (Final,

61–62); 3 v. Torquay United (64–65); 3 v. Ipswich Town (64–65); 1 v. Preston (65–66); 1 v. Portsmouth (66–67); 2 v. Bristol City (66–67); 2 v. Birmingham City (66–67); 1 v. Nottingham Forest (semi-final, 66–67); 2 v. Preston (67–68); 1 v. Liverpool (67–68); 1 v. Walsall (68–69); 1 v. Wolves (68–69); 2 v. Aston Villa (68–69); 3 v. Bradford City (69–70).

His League Cup goals haul was 7:

FOR CHELSEA – 2 v. Millwall (60–61).

FOR SPURS – 3 v. Exeter City (68–69), 1 v. Peterborough United (68–69), 1 v. Arsenal (68–69).

He scored 9 goals for AC Milan in 14 appearances, 10 European Cup Winners' Cup goals, 3 in the Fairs Cup, 6 in Inter-League matches, 2 in the Charity Shield, 2 for England v. Young England, 2 for the Rest of Europe team and 1 for England v. the Football League.

His total goals in all matches at the time of his retirement from League football in 1971 was *491*.

He scored 44 goals in 57 full England internationals. Only Bobby Charlton (49 in 106 matches) has scored more. His 13 goals in 12 England Under-23 international matches is a record.

These are the countries against which Jimmy scored his 44 international goals:

1959: Peru (1), Wales (1); 1960: Yugoslavia (1), Northern Ireland (2), Luxembourg (3), Spain (1), Wales (2); 1961: Scotland (3), Italy (1), Austria (1); 1962: Peru (3), Argentina (1), Northern Ireland (1), Wales (1); 1963: Czechoslovakia (2), Wales (1), Rest of the World (1),

Northern Ireland (4); 1964: Eire (1), Brazil (1), Northern Ireland (3), Holland (1); 1965: Scotland (1), Hungary (1); 1966: Yugoslavia (1), Norway (4); 1967: Spain (1).

He played his first League game for Chelsea against Tottenham at White Hart Lane on 23 August 1957. *And scored*. He made his debut for England Under-23s against Bulgaria at Stamford Bridge on 25 September 1957. *And scored twice*. He made his full international debut for England against Peru in Lima on 17 May 1959. *And scored*. He made his debut for AC Milan against Botafogo in the San Siro stadium on 7 June 1961. *And scored*. He made his debut for Tottenham against Blackpool at White Hart Lane on 16 December 1961. *And scored a hat-trick*. He played in his first FA Cup Final for Spurs against Burnley at Wembley on 4 May 1962. *And scored*. He made his debut for West Ham against Manchester City at Upton Park on 20 March 1970. *And scored two goals*.

At 21, Jimmy became the youngest player to score 100 League goals. At 23 years and 290 days he scored his 200th League goal, which was exactly the same age at which Dixie Dean had reached the milestone with Everton.

His most prolific goal-scoring season was with Chelsea in 1956–7 while still an apprentice professional. He scored 114 goals and Chelsea presented him with an illuminated address to mark the feat. On the first day of the following season he made his League debut ...

JIMMY'S 357 LEAGUE GOALS

Table compiled by Harry Cook, Soccer Statistician of the *Daily Express*

	CHELSEA					TOTTENHAM							W. HAM		
	57–58	58–59	59–60	60–61	61–62	62–63	63–64	64–65	65–66	66–67	67–68	68–69	69–70	70–71	TOTAL
ARSENAL	2	1	0	1	0	0	2	1	0	2	0	1	1	0	**11**
ASTON VILLA	3	2		2	2	2	3			0					**11**
BIRMINGHAM CITY	3	1	2	1	2	0	4	2	2	0		0			**17**
BLACKBURN ROVERS			0	3	2	2	4	2					1		**14**
BLACKPOOL	2	0	0	3	3	2	4	1	2		3			0	**18**
BOLTON	0	0	0	1		1	2			2	0				**5**
BURNLEY	1	1	1	3	0		1	1	0	1	3	3	1	0	**19**
CARDIFF CITY				2	1			0		1	0	1		0	**2**
CHELSEA											4		0	0	**4**
COVENTRY CITY										1		0		0	**5**
DERBY COUNTY				2				2	0		0		0		**2**
EVERTON	2	1	1	1	1	0	0	2	0	1	0	1			**11**
FULHAM		3	0			4	2	2	0	2	0		1	2	**12**
IPSWICH TOWN							1	1	2	2		0	1	0	**10**
LEEDS UNITED	0	2	0	3	2	3		3	2	2		3		1	**15**
LEICESTER CITY	0	1	0	4	2	4	0	1	0	2	1	2	0		**11**
LIVERPOOL														2	**2**
LUTON TOWN	0	0	2	3	2	2		0	1	0	2	0	2	0	**17**
MANCHESTER CITY	0	2	3	0	2	3			0	0	0	0	2	0	**13**
MANCHESTER UNITED	1	2	2	4			1		1	2	0	2	2	0	**13**
NEWCASTLE UNITED		4	1		0	4	4	1	0		1	2	1		**1**
NORTHAMPTON						1				2					**1**
NOTTINGHAM FOREST	0			4		4	4		0	2					**24**
ORIENT															**1**
PORTSMOUTH	4	1													**5**

															TOTAL
PRESTON	0	2	8	0											10
QPR													-		1
SOUTHAMPTON					-	2	0	2	0	-	2	2	-	0	6
SHEFFIELD UNITED	3		0	0	2	0	0	2	0	2	2				9
SHEFFIELD WED.	0						2	-	-	0	-	0	0		8
STOKE CITY	-	-						2	-	-	0	-	0	-	7
SUNDERLAND	-	0	-	-	0	0	2			-	2	4	0		10
TOTTENHAM		3	2	5	0	3	0	-	2					-	5
WEST BROMWICH A.	-	5	0	-	0	2	2	3	0	0	0	2	0	-	16
WEST HAM	1		0	3	0		2	0		2	2	2	0		16
WOLVES											2	0	-	0	16
TOTAL	22	32	29	41	21	37	35	29	15	25	23	27	12	9	357

Appendix 2

The games Jimmy played

These are the results of the 57 matches in which Jimmy played for England and the forward lines in which he appeared. The figures in brackets are the goals that he scored:

Year	Opponents	Venue	Result	7	8	9	10	11
1959	Peru	Lima	1–4	Deeley	Greaves (1)	Charlton	Haynes	Holden
1959	Mexico	Mexico City	1–2	Holden*	Greaves	Kevan	Haynes	Charlton
1959	USA	Los Angeles	8–1	Bradley	Greaves	Kevan	Haynes	Charlton
1959	Wales	Cardiff	1–1	Connelly	Greaves (1)	Clough	Charlton	Holliday
1959	Sweden	Wembley	2–3	Connelly	Greaves	Clough	Charlton	Holliday
1960	Yugoslavia	Wembley	3–3	Douglas	Haynes	Baker	Greaves (1)	Charlton
1960	Spain	Madrid	0–3	Brabrook	Haynes	Baker	Greaves	Charlton
1960	N. Ireland	Belfast	5–2	Douglas	Greaves (2)	Smith	Haynes	Charlton
1960	Luxembourg	Luxembourg	9–0	Douglas	Greaves (3)	Smith	Haynes	Charlton
1960	Spain	Wembley	4–2	Douglas	Greaves (1)	Smith	Haynes	Charlton
1960	Wales	Wembley	5–1	Douglas	Greaves (2)	Smith	Haynes	Charlton
1961	Scotland	Wembley	9–3	Douglas	Greaves (3)	Smith	Haynes	Charlton
1961	Portugal	Lisbon	1–1	Douglas	Greaves	Smith	Haynes	Charlton
1961	Italy	Rome	3–2	Douglas	Greaves (1)	Hitchens	Haynes	Charlton
1961	Austria	Vienna	1–3	Douglas	Greaves (1)	Hitchens	Haynes	Charlton
1962	Scotland	Glasgow	0–2	Douglas	Greaves	Smith	Haynes	Charlton
1962	Switzerland	Wembley	3–1	Connelly	Greaves	Hitchens	Haynes	Charlton
1962	Peru	Lima	4–0	Douglas	Greaves (3)	Hitchens	Haynes	Charlton
1962	Hungary‡	Rancaqua	1–2	Douglas	Greaves	Hitchens	Haynes	Charlton
1962	Argentina‡	Rancaqua	3–1	Douglas	Greaves (1)	Peacock	Haynes	Charlton
1962	Bulgaria‡	Rancaqua	0–0	Douglas	Greaves	Peacock	Haynes	Charlton
1962	Brazil‡	Vina del Mar	1–3	Douglas	Greaves	Hitchens	Haynes	Charlton
1962	France	Hillsborough	1–1	Hellawell	Crowe	Charnley	Greaves	Hinton
1962	N. Ireland	Belfast	3–1	Hellawell	Hill	Peacock	Greaves (1)	O'Grady
1962	Wales	Wembley	4–0	Connelly	Hill	Peacock	Greaves (1)	Tambling
1963	France†	Paris	2–5	Connelly	Tambling	Smith	Greaves	Charlton
1963	Scotland	Wembley	1–2	Douglas	Greaves	Smith	Melia	Charlton
1963	Brazil	Wembley	1–1	Douglas	Greaves	Smith	Eastham	Charlton
1963	Czechoslovakia	Bratislava	4–2	Paine	Greaves (2)	Smith	Eastham	Charlton

1963	Switzerland	Basle	8-1	Douglas	Greaves	Byrne	Melia	Charlton
1963	Wales	Cardiff	4-0	Paine	Greaves (1)	Smith	Eastham	Charlton
1963	Rest of World	Wembley	2-1	Paine	Greaves (1)	Smith	Eastham	Charlton
1963	N. Ireland	Wembley	8-3	Paine	Greaves (4)	Smith	Eastham	Charlton
1964	Uruguay	Wembley	2-1	Paine	Greaves	Byrne	Eastham	Charlton
1964	Portugal	Lisbon	4-3	Thompson	Greaves	Byrne	Eastham	Charlton
1964	Eire	Dublin	3-1	Thompson	Greaves (1)	Byrne	Eastham	Charlton
1964	Brazil	Rio de Janeiro	1-5	Thompson	Greaves (1)	Byrne	Eastham	Charlton
1964	Portugal	Sao Paulo	1-1	Paine	Greaves	Byrne	Hunt	Thompson
1964	Argentina	Rio de Janeiro	0-1	Thompson	Greaves	Byrne	Eastham	Charlton
1964	N. Ireland	Belfast	4-3	Paine	Greaves (3)	Pickering	Charlton	Thompson
1964	Belgium	Wembley	2-2	Thompson	Greaves	Pickering	Venables	Hinton
1964	Netherlands	Amsterdam	1-1	Thompson	Greaves (1)	Wignall	Venables	Charlton
1965	Scotland	Wembley	2-2	Thompson	Greaves (1)	Bridges	Byrne	Charlton
1965	Hungary	Wembley	1-0	Paine	Greaves (1)	Bridges	Eastham	Connelly
1965	Yugoslavia	Belgrade	1-1	Paine	Greaves	Bridges	Ball	Connelly
1965	Wales	Cardiff	0-0	Paine	Greaves	Peacock	Charlton	Connelly
1965	Austria	Wembley	2-3	Paine	Greaves	Bridges	Charlton	Connelly
1966	Yugoslavia	Wembley	2-0	Paine	Greaves (1)	Charlton	Hurst	Tambling
1966	Norway	Oslo	6-1	Paine	Greaves (4)	Charlton	Hunt	Connelly
1966	Denmark	Copenhagen	2-0	Ball	Greaves	Hurst	Eastham	Connelly
1966	Poland	Chorzhow	1-0	Ball	Greaves	Charlton	Hunt	Peters
1966	Uruguay‡	Wembley	0-0	Ball	Greaves	Charlton	Hunt	Connelly
1966	Mexico‡	Wembley	2-0	Paine	Greaves	Charlton	Hunt	Peters
1966	France‡	Wembley	2-0	Callaghan	Greaves	Charlton	Hunt	Peters
1967	Scotland	Wembley	2-3	Ball	Greaves	Charlton	Hurst	Peters
1967	Spain	Wembley	2-0	Ball	Greaves (1)	Hurst	Hunt	Hollins
1967	Austria	Vienna	1-0	Ball	Greaves	Hurst	Hunt	Hunter

SUMMARY:
Games played 57; Won 30; Lost 14; Drawn 13;
Goals scored 44.

* Bradley substituted second-half.
† First match under Alf Ramsey's management.
‡ World Cup matches.

Index

Index

Index